The Feedback-Friendly Classroom

How to equip students to give, receive, and
seek quality feedback that will support their social,
academic, and developmental needs

Deborah McCallum

Pembroke Publishers Limited

© 2015 Pembroke Publishers
538 Hood Road
Markham, Ontario, Canada L3R 3K9
www.pembrokepublishers.com

Distributed in the U.S. by Stenhouse Publishers
480 Congress Street
Portland, ME 04101
www.stenhouse.com

Library and Archives Canada Cataloguing in Publication

McCallum, Deborah, author
    The feedback-friendly classroom / Deborah McCallum.

Includes bibliographical references and index.
Issued in print and electronic formats.
ISBN 978-1-55138-304-0 (paperback).--ISBN 978-1-55138-908-0 (pdf)

    1. Communication in education. 2. Teacher-student relationships. 3. Feedback (Psychology). 4. Education, Elementary. I. Title.

LB1033.5.M43 2015   371.102'2   C2015-903644-5
                                          C2015-903645-3

Editor: Kat Mototsune
Cover Design: John Zehethofer
Typesetting: Jay Tee Graphics Ltd.

Printed and bound in Canada
9 8 7 6 5 4 3 2 1

Contents

Introduction

There was a time when feedback seemed to me like an extra task that needed to be completed on top of everything else in my classroom. My mindset about feedback centred around mostly the formal aspects of feedback as connected to an assessment. It also was connected to more informal aspects of feedback carved out by specific teacher-planned tasks, including one-on-one conferences and helping with tips and questions as I circulated the classroom. In a nutshell, there was no co-creation or customization of a feedback culture. Except for activities specifically organized to help students engage in a peer or self-assessment, feedback was something that I, as the teacher, fully controlled.

But I've come to understand that feedback is a vital part of teaching and learning processes. Feedback is possibly the most important variable that improves student performance; increasing the feedback that students receive invariably increases student achievement. Students need feedback to understand how to work toward learning goals and curricular outcomes. In this sense, it becomes a significant roadmap for thinking and learning. Practical feedback strategies help students improve learning, and we need to ensure that more students are receiving meaningful feedback in the classroom. The process of learning with feedback is so much more than a part of evaluation and assessment; it is the underlying foundation of all learning.

As educators, we often perceive barriers to giving meaningful feedback in the classroom. Regular and ongoing feedback can feel like an extra task we just don't have time for. We tend to have our set ways of organizing our classrooms and managing our time. These restrictions combine with personal beliefs that we might hold about feedback (van den Bergh, 2013). Also, we often associate feedback only with assessment. Feedback relates to assessment *for*, *as*, and *of* learning; however, feedback does not need to be synonymous with assessment. Traditional school paradigms have reinforced the idea that feedback is comprised of the official texts that accompany assessments and is best delivered by the teacher to students. However, feedback can be a much larger process that permeates the classroom. While feedback is essential to the learning process, it does not need to be limited to formative oral and written texts from the teacher. Students have key roles to play in the feedback processes that take place within the classroom.

In fact, we can change traditional schemata of feedback to encompass holistic strategies that our students can get involved with each day. Our students are

How do we know if our students are learning more from feedback from the teacher than from feedback from their peers?

powerful sources of information for each other and, by harnessing feedback in processes outside of assessment, we can create a feedback-friendly classroom that promotes effective socialization, academics, and development.

Students share valuable feedback with each other on a daily basis. In fact, according to Nuthall (2007), most of the feedback that students receive comes from their peers, and most of that feedback is incorrect. Wow! What an epiphany, that 80% of the feedback my students are receiving is not coming from me, and likely not even correct. I began to think that this could have very profound implications for student self-esteem, peer relationships, growth mindsets, and the ability of students to accomplish the learning goals.

As a teacher in a classroom of students with diverse and unique learning needs, clearly my students were receiving feedback, whether I was a part of it or not. But what could I do about it? I knew that I could not be everywhere at once; I could not give feedback to everyone at once. How would I have time to teach? But I knew I had to get more valuable, timely, and meaningful feedback to my students. How could I affect changes in the feedback that students give each other? Should I give more peer assessment worksheets? Increase my use of communication strategies? Use more technology? I realized that I had to think about my whole school day and instructional design differently.

One of the things that I quickly came to see was that, as educators, we cannot simply increase the feedback already in place. As John Hattie (2009) points out, we should be concerned about merely starting to give students the task of increasing peer feedback. It is not just about increasing the feedback opportunities, but also about increasing the quality of feedback that is being shared. I really wanted to make sure that classroom feedback was effective for learning. How could feedback be harnessed to permeate the interactions of the classroom in ways that would create a feedback-friendly classroom? I could come up with many different strategies. However, I had to wonder what would make those strategies successful. It was clear that I needed to regularly teach, model, and implement key strategies that create safe classroom environments. I also needed strategies that would promote growth mindsets, allow for errors, and consist of goals that would be appropriately challenging for all the different types of learners.

There are many forms of assessment that give us feedback about our students and also help us provide meaningful feedback to our students. But what about the interactions and learning that are accomplished outside of assessment? What about the feedback that teachers and students receive on a daily basis that we take for granted because it is not embedded within assessment for, of, and as learning procedures? These are the kinds of questions that kept me up at night. They are also the questions that led me to consider the idea that feedback is a continuous process that students need to use to engage with each other and with us each day. If we are not acknowledging the ongoing feedback that is already taking place, then what kind of damage could be happening to the learning and assessment processes that are taking place in the classroom? Could it be sabotaging the hard work that I was doing for the students? If we think about feedback as a process that is not solely connected with assessment, we open ourselves up to viewing it as any communication that helps our students self-regulate, improve, grow, move toward learning goals, and become good citizens and critical thinkers.

We can harness the feedback opportunities that daily present themselves. The thing is, this requires a classroom culture of trust, honesty, and collaboration. Each classroom and learning environment relies on teachers to facilitate the conversations, behaviors, beliefs, and strategies that lead to higher-quality feedback to promote learning and achievement. We can embed our ongoing feedback directly into the fabric of the entire classroom ecosystem, and help students develop the skills they need to survive as we continue to move deeper into the 21st century.

What are those 21st-century skills that effective feedback-friendly classrooms promote? Feedback-friendly classrooms promote participatory cultures that allow students themselves to develop agency in what they are learning. Classrooms that are feedback-friendly also promote learner agency, provide constructivist and active learning opportunities, integrate subjects and learning skills, are inquiry-based, and are open to what students need to learn and grow. Feedback-friendly classrooms allow students to express safely their opinions, views, languages, and cultures, and to construct their knowledge and meaning from the interactions. They promote knowledge-building and growth mindsets and teach students that there are no ending points to learning. Feedback-friendly classrooms help students develop the skills they will need to participate fully in a globalized world. Our ability to embrace and share emerging values of our world societies is contingent on our ability to give, receive, and seek feedback. Our world is connected and highly networked, and feedback is a key literacy of the 21st century. Learning ways to give, receive, and seek quality feedback will enhance not only the classroom learning environment but also our communications and learning within a networked world.

Feedback is a process that is ongoing, and that requires everyone's voice to move it forward. A feedback-friendly environment allows us to focus more on students than on assessment as the sole means of conveying feedback. Feedback, therefore, becomes a process that students are actively engaged in. It is not a separate activity that is imposed on students. Each day we are evolving individually and collectively as a classroom culture to meet our socialization, academic, and developmental needs.

1

Understanding Feedback

Feedback as Principle and Process

As educators we often view feedback solely as a principle, as something that we as teachers impart to students to help them achieve desired outcomes. It is this principle that guides students to take the necessary steps to achieve favourable outcomes. The teacher directs, instructs, and imparts knowledge and feedback to the student; the student then follows this feedback to achieve the highest outcomes possible. As a principle, feedback becomes viewed as a cause-and-effect variable. The feedback is the cause and student outcomes are the effect.

When we view feedback as a principle, we risk blaming the giver of the feedback when students fail to achieve the set standards. The teacher becomes the sole active variable when it comes to feedback. Also, it becomes impossible for students to affect teaching outcomes. In this "learning" paradigm where feedback is a principle, students have no voice. We fail to recognize student backgrounds, knowledge, experiences, cultures, and learning needs.

Feedback viewed solely as a principle can snowball. More and more individualized and personalized feedback needs to be disseminated and shared with students. Feedback starts to feel like more work that we don't have time for because of all of the teaching we still have to do. It can feel like we spend our nights writing feedback on assessments, and our days in conferences with students. As time goes on, feedback as a principle gets strongly reinforced. Feedback from this point of view can feel like, look like, and sound like a full-time job that must be performed by the teacher in the classroom, and must result in high student achievement.

Certainly, feedback as a principle is important and has appropriate uses in the context of traditional assessments. Feedback is obviously a natural extension of assessment that we cannot ignore, and that does indeed have positive effects on student learning. However, we can extend our understanding of feedback beyond the boundaries of principles and move toward the interconnected processes that have great value in learning.

Feedback is also a process. In fact, it is one of the most powerful processes—if not the most powerful process—we can use to enhance learning. Conceptually, feedback looks and acts differently as a process than it does as a principle. When we view feedback as a process, it becomes interrelated and multi-faceted;

it incorporates many decisions from many people. The fact is that feedback processes are going on all the time within our classrooms. It is up to us as educators to harness these processes to propel learning forward in meaningful ways. If we look at feedback and fail to see the interactive processes at play, then we fail to understand and harness these powerful networks of communication.

In the process of feedback, feedback principles inform and illuminate learning processes. As a process, feedback is continuous. It involves a series of strategies, steps, and mindsets that help students learn. All students have the capacity to learn, and they do learn, regardless of "appropriate" standards. It starts to be about *when* learning will happen and *how* it will happen, not *if* it will happen. The ongoing feedback process built into a feedback-friendly classroom is essential to facilitating this learning. The feedback process should help all members of the classroom bridge the distance between what they currently know and what we want them to learn.

See the graphic on page 11 for a series of steps that make up the feedback process.

See The Feedback Process graphic on page 11.

In the visual, you can see that the feedback process includes not only the variables of teacher-to-student or student-to-student interaction, but also how student feedback can feed forward to the teacher to influence lesson planning and instructional design. It highlights the processes by which a teacher can extract feedback from student learning, behaviors, assessments, and comments, and can translate this into future learning. It also can be applied to students, and interpreted through well-implemented strategies for students to help each other and improve each other's learning in meaningful ways. As participants of learning within a classroom, we can take this valuable information and feedback and make key decisions on where to go next, because we are all working together.

Feedback is not an end in and of itself, but part of ongoing and interrelated processes. These processes are essential to learning activities and success criteria, and build relationships by weaving together the skills, social interactions, learning goals, and cultures within a classroom environment. It links essential information, literacy skills, digital citizenship, learning skills, and overall expectations, just to name a few components of learning. It enhances and validates student voice, homes in on information literacy skills, and helps students to think critically and manipulate information for new learning.

Feedback and Assessment

As educators, we are accountable for increasing student achievement, and this inevitably needs to be measured through assessment. Feedback is invariably linked with assessment processes. But assessment is an evaluation strategy that provides a snapshot of student learning at one point in time. By contrast, feedback has the potential to bridge learning gaps in student academics, socialization, and development. It goes beyond assessment in that it has great potential to be non-evaluative.

A lot of people equate feedback with assessment. In fact, we often define feedback as what we share with students after they have finished a task or a test that has been marked. In this view, feedback is merely an extension of the assessment piece or the grade that has been handed out. Giving more and regular feedback to students can feel like an extra duty or a task that there simply is not enough time for. We ask ourselves, *When would teaching happen if we were giving out*

The Feedback Process

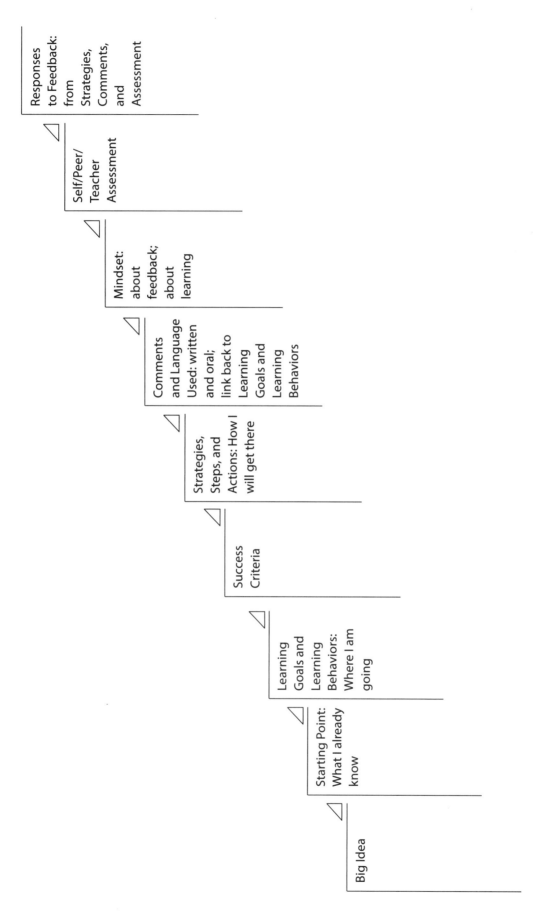

Responses to Feedback: from Strategies, Comments, and Assessment

Self/Peer/ Teacher Assessment

Mindset: about feedback; about learning

Comments and Language Used: written and oral; link back to Learning Goals and Learning Behaviors

Strategies, Steps, and Actions: How I will get there

Success Criteria

Learning Goals and Learning Behaviors: Where I am going

Starting Point: What I already know

Big Idea

more feedback on a regular basis? This question has embedded assumptions about feedback being exclusively tied to assessment practices. It warrants a shift in mindset away from assessment as the only way to give feedback. We can move toward a feedback-friendly classroom where teachers and students are harnessing social strategies each day to gain quantitative and qualitative feedback for learning and instruction.

Assessment is often used as a basis for the development of our lessons, units, and programming. It provides important feedback in and of itself, and can happen at the beginning, middle, or end of a lesson or unit. However, if we are not careful, assessment can become the driver of our pedagogical practices, when in reality we want feedback to play that driving role in teaching instead. To be meaningful, feedback needs to be ongoing and constant, and students need to be able to work with it. Its validity does not rely solely on its use in assessment initiatives. Its validity comes from how students use it and how meaningful we can make it. Further, we need to leverage the feedback we observe and receive to improve and realign our instructional practices with the learning needs of students.

Feedback between students is also crucial to learning; to regard feedback only in terms of teacher-run assessment would be to ignore the power of the social relationships in the classroom. Each day, students get significant information from each other in terms of answers, procedures, and directions. Nuthall (2007) demonstrated that spontaneous peer talk is a self-generated learning experience in the classroom. This spontaneous talk is not required and, as we know, arises from the activities and learning goals we give to students. We often do not stop to consider the true power of these social relationships within the classroom. Spontaneous conversations have tremendous potential to contribute to the content that students learn. What Nuthall tries to encapsulate is that much of the knowledge students learn from each other is actually wrapped inside the social relationships of the classroom. He goes on to discuss how social relationships change constantly, and how students have to spend time in class maintaining them and changing them. Therefore, the world of the classroom contains much more than the content of the curriculum. As assessment pertains to content, feedback encapsulates assessment and learning via social relationships and personal development.

As more and more schools use computers to employ formative assessment to students, it is important to point out that the technology cannot replace the teacher or the social relationships in the classroom. Regardless of how technology-enabled a classroom is, that it is feedback-friendly is more important. In fact, with tech-enabled computer assessments and computer-based formative feedback, it is even more important for students and teachers alike to become highly involved in the feedback processes. To this extent, technology can actually humanize the teaching–learning process (Ornstein, 2013). Computerized formative feedback does not mean that we abandon traditional anecdotal records, checklists, journals, and other templates for feedback. Observations and conversations need to be equally utilized as part of the assessment of the products. What is most important is that students and teachers can use feedback processes to understand the values and goals of the classroom community and learners.

Consider the following Top Ten points of feedback relationship to assessment (adapted from The Quality Assurance Agency for Higher Education, 2009):

Often, when we think of feedback, we think of evaluation and assessment. But the process of learning with feedback is not something that is measured in standardized tests.

Feedback and technology meet in digital environments, including online book clubs, social media, and Web 2.0- or Web 3.0-related spaces where students can connect, give, receive, and seek valuable feedback in digital worlds that extend beyond the four walls of the classroom.

Good feedback should

1. Clarify what good performance is as it pertains to academics, socialization, and development, and provide ample opportunities to engage with strategies before, during, and after assessment.
2. Encourage deep vs. surface learning. Students interact with learning goals to make key connections and enhance learning through other feedback comprehension strategies.
3. Be interacted with regularly. Good feedback is not just given once and acted upon; it is regularly interacted with by teachers and students. To this extent, we can view it as a driver for learning, and not a measurement of learning.
4. Align with formative and summative assessments; i.e., assessment for, as, and of learning processes.
5. Promote peer dialogue around assessments.
6. Be reflected on.
7. Inform student choice for choosing topics, building success criteria, and making decisions.
8. Support socialization and classroom learning communities.
9. Enhance student motivation and self-esteem.
10. Feed forward to the adapting, planning, and differentiation of further strategies and opportunities in class.

In a feedback-friendly classroom, we are building productive learning cultures where students get to develop their skills, learn new ideas from others, and feel safe to take risks and make mistakes in a non-judgmental environment. The idea that students should receive feedback only in the context of assessment needs to change. We can mobilize the feedback that is already happening in our classrooms to anchor individual learning to classroom goals, routines, strategies, and learning expectations. In this way, we can also work toward identifying the specific needs of each unique learning environment and promote real differentiation that goes beyond assessment toward nonevaluative feedback.

Feedback and the Growth Mindset

We are hearing a lot these days about mindsets in education. Your mindset is a cognitive schema, a mental set that determines how you will organize, understand, and respond to a given situation. In education, we have mindsets that connect with what we think learning and education should be. We have mindsets regarding feedback as well. Some of these mindsets come from traditional views of what we think school should be. A lot of the mindsets that permeate our modern education system include the idea that we are in school to get good grades. The unfortunate thing about grades is that they promote fixed mindsets (Dweck, 2006). They hinder a student's ability to give and receive feedback, and can put undue pressure on the teacher to focus on grades instead of helping students make mistakes and learn from them. According to Carol Dweck, students with a fixed mindset do not believe that they can improve and get better beyond what their brains and behaviors can accomplish. A fixed mindset could look like a student giving up on the learning process after they have made a mistake. A fixed mindset also could look like a student striving to maintain an A and to "look smart" instead of taking risks to engage in new inquiries and try new skills.

We need to let students know that learning is not something that people do well in or poorly in, but that learning will indeed happen, regardless of how the learning goals are met or not met.

With a growth mindset, students inherently understand that they can achieve. Students with growth mindsets are appropriately challenged with their work to grow and learn because learning is going to happen. It is important that we don't push students too far or too hard, as this will only promote a fixed mindset. If our feedback tells students that they just have not met the learning goals, and provides no hints for improvement, then students will believe that they cannot get better, that they cannot reach the success criteria and learning goals. Our feedback needs to appropriately acknowledge the learning that students have already demonstrated and provide explicit descriptive feedback for students to continue to improve. This is the only way to foster a growth mindset in students.

A Growth Mindset for Teaching

We all come to the classroom with our own beliefs about how people learn. We have our own theories about ethnicity, culture, learning styles, academics, development, and how to achieve in the classroom. We still need to make sure that we are doing our best to create positive learning conditions for all students. Regardless of our beliefs, it helps everyone when we believe that all students can and will learn. We help students develop multiple styles of learning and multiple problem-solving strategies that they can use in their repertoires. Our feedback strategies can promote this, without negating the implementation of learning goals and success criteria. Challenging goals must be set for students, as well as new feedback and learning mindsets

A fixed mindset views the path to learning as linear. This mindset worked in the Industrial Era, when the skills and knowledge we needed were directly related to the products being made and sold in a product-based economy. But we now live in a knowledge economy. Today's world is no longer stable and linear, where we will learn fixed skill sets to use in one job for our whole career. Technology provides unprecedented access to information and ways to interact with that information, to add to it, to share it, to manipulate it in ways that humans never have been able to in the past. Giving, receiving, and seeking appropriate feedback, and then knowing what to do about it, is perhaps one of the most important skill sets our students will need as they embark on their career paths.

We need to structure our classroom and activities to acquire diagnostic information about what students know, to learn what they think about and what is important to them. We can organize and embed opportunities in our feedback strategies to help students learn that not everyone thinks in the same way; this is especially important for younger students. We can use feedback strategies to help students understand *how* they think instead of *what* they are thinking about. Growth mindsets point us in the direction of *how* students are going to learn and integrate new information, rather than *what* they are going to learn.

We can help students to identify their feedback mindset and help prescribe key vocabulary, language, and strategies to begin the process of changing our feedback mindsets.

A Growth Mindset for Learning

Learning is messy. It does not follow linear paths, and students do not all come to the table with the same level of readiness, willingness, and other factors that help them learn at optimal levels. Learning should be challenging. If it is too easy, our students cannot develop growth mindsets for learning. On the other hand, if learning is too hard, it will not occur. An appropriate amount of struggle could very well be the key ingredient for making learning challenging at just the right levels. However, in a fixed mindset, *struggling* is sometimes seen as synonymous

Consider our gifted students, or students with multiple diagnoses, autism, processing and executive functioning issues, LDs, visual and auditory impairments, and more. All students require appropriate challenges and appropriate opportunities to struggle.

with *failing*. At the first sign of struggle, students feel like they should give up, or that it is just not possible for them to learn, get the grade, or meet the success criteria. Students might learn that if they struggle too much and are still struggling at the end of the math literacy block, then learning opportunities are over.

Feedback can help students and teachers to harness the struggle as a natural part of how we achieve in the world. The goal is not to help students avoid struggle, but to help them move through it. Then our job is to help them see the learning they have done. When students can see that they have indeed harnessed their struggles, and indeed have learned, a growth mindset can flourish to help students through the next struggle.

Research demonstrates that when we praise children for performance, they value the performance itself more than the process (Dweck, 2006); i.e., they value the actual task more than their interests and motivations. And why wouldn't they? It is human nature to respond and learn based on reinforcements, and feedback is a strong way to reinforce behaviors, including conforming behaviors.

We want to avoid empty praise and instead focus on giving valuable information about what has gone well and why. In fact, research shows that descriptive feedback is more helpful than evaluative feedback that simply informs students about how well they did (Anastasyia & Smith, 2009). It has been established that detailed, descriptive feedback is the most effective when given alone, without a grade or praise. Further, descriptive feedback leads to the highest levels of achievement. (Black, 1998)

We need to change feedback processes from a judging standpoint to one of understanding (Masters, 2014); we need to change our mindset about what feedback is. As Carol Dweck said:

> When [teachers and students] change to a growth mindset, they change from a judge-and-be-judged framework to a learn-and-help-learn framework. Their commitment is to growth, and growth takes plenty of time, effort and mutual support (Dweck, 2006: 244).

One of our biggest fears, as human beings, is being rejected. In our traditional school system, students can feel rejected if peers are putting down students, their efforts, and their outcomes (i.e., their grades). What students need is an environment where mistakes are accepted and encouraged, an environment that uses feedback in meaningful ways to help students develop a growth mindset about their mistakes. We can use feedback to help instill this sense that students can grow and get better, and that they are always accepted for who they are.

Feedback is going to take place throughout our classrooms whether we acknowledge it or not. Therefore, we can harness our strategies not merely to teach the effective ways to give and receive feedback, but also to build a sense of trust and safety. When trust is enhanced, students feel safe to make mistakes on their learning path. As a result, they will also feel safer to take risks and push their learning; feedback is more likely to be given in meaningful ways, and also accepted and sought in meaningful ways; students will inevitably develop growth mindsets.

MindsetWorks© at http://www.mindsetworks.com/free-resources/ has many free resources that you can use in the classroom to promote growth mindsets.

Feedback and Community-Building

Feedback can be used to build learning communities. Students work not only to make the classroom a feedback-friendly place, but also to use feedback strategies to build a stronger learning community. Each classroom community will differ according to different variables, especially in terms of varying degrees of participation, creation, and implementation of feedback strategies for socialization, academics, and development. While all stakeholders—students, parents, outer community, administrators, and more—may want the best for our students, we all likely have different ideas about what the best is. Therefore, the community comes together and gains strength through the feedback strategies used. We all need to work together to share feedback beyond the classrooms with parents and other peers and more. Strategies include the use of various technologies, feedback information nights for parents, and homework being directly linked to sharing feedback for learning in the classroom.

Strong feedback-friendly classroom communities need trust to be successful. As a classroom, we can move beyond the teacher-helping-student model to create a culture of ongoing feedback. We can create an environment where students learn to internalize the dialogue, questions, curiosities, observations, and reflections that are conduits for propelling their learning, and also to support one another in this process. It is only when students can support other students and recognize that there are other strategies, viewpoints, styles, and voices that we can truly begin to appreciate the complexities of learning. We must always remember that a great amount of student feedback comes from peers, body language, classroom organization, and casual verbalizations. Feedback is not merely what the teacher says to a student.

We want students to go beyond just doing the activities—questioning, problem-solving, inquiry-based learning—to move past hearing their thoughts and wonderings. We want them to notice the key features of events and activities and make connections between their thoughts and wonderings and what others are wondering as well. The feedback that promotes the identification of patterns, possibilities, alternative points of view, creating plans, self-monitoring, identification of bias, setting priorities, and testing hypotheses is feedback that builds a community of learners.

Helping students uncover their abilities and learn how to harness them for learning sets the frameworks for a successful feedback community. These frameworks are flexible and have the ability to evolve over time. They provide boundaries that help organize the patterns of learning and communication within the classroom learning environment. They also help to set the stage for the evolution of effective feedback processes that will help drive the learning forward from teacher to student, and from student to student.

"Does this contribute to a sense of loss for many students when they do finally walk out of the doors of our educational institutions for the last time? Or does it give them a sense of security that they can be contributing and loyal members of society?" — Carol Dweck (2006)

2

Feedback for Learning

Feedback infuses all interactions. But much of the communication that takes place in a classroom is unreliable. It is still true that feedback is about timely, explicit, and relevant information that aids in learning. However, if most of the feedback is, in fact, happening between peers, then we need to think deeper about how to harness the strategies and tools that will help them give better feedback that drives learning. Feedback becomes the threads that bring together all of our classroom interactions that influence student learning.

The reality is that we are obtaining feedback about others and our environment on a regular basis in our classrooms. How we facilitate these interactions to support higher-quality feedback will ultimately determine the richness of learning that can take place in a classroom. When we can make meaningful changes to the social interactions within a classroom, we can improve the feedback that is already occurring in our classrooms, enhancing daily social interactions so that they are supportive of feedback for learning.

Feedback is ultimately more than merely knowing the results to improve future learning. Students also need to understand how to, when to, and when not to use information. This is largely accomplished through feedback gleaned through interpersonal relationships within the classroom. This kind of learning occurs in real-time conversations within a classroom. Key evidence from our social interactions will show us the kinds of feedback students are already sharing with each other every day. We can surmise that the effectiveness of the feedback will be determined by the social contexts of the classroom.

The feedback-friendly classroom is based on the assumption that learning is inherently social. It is a paradigm we can harness to help students take their social interactions to new levels to promote meaningful relationships, deep thinking, and collaboration; to help them think about learning goals, their personal strengths, and weaknesses; to show how they can help others and how to ask effective questions. All of this goes toward building safe and effective learning relationships.

High-quality relationships are the cornerstone of the feedback-friendly classroom. They promote effective feedback processes that help us scaffold learning toward appropriate learning goals. This scaffolding often necessitates the use of differentiated strategies; i.e., learning will look different depending on the relationships of students and where students are at in their learning. Many of our overall expectations within the curriculum are basically the same from grade to grade, providing the opportunity to think more deeply about the expectations and concepts with only slight variations; however, feedback allows learning to be structured in flexible ways, using rich learning tasks that provide multiple points of entry to reach the learning goals. For example, one student might be on an IEP (Individual Education Plan) for vision impairment, another might not be working at grade level, and yet another could be on an IEP for giftedness and require acceleration. With rich tasks that incorporate interaction and feedback throughout the entire process, we provide opportunities for students to take risks, work toward their strengths, and meet the learning goals in ways that are appropriate for them. The strategies to interact with the tasks are not simple, nor are they closed and exclusive to certain individuals. They are open-ended, and allow students to follow their inquiries, interests, and learning needs, to attack the problems and learning tasks from different points of entry. The learning goals we create from the feedback we get from our students can be met by each because the rich task allows that student to express learning in appropriate ways.

Learner Variables

It is important to teach our students to recognize that everyone's knowledge and experience are essential parts of the learning processes.

Feedback can become the conversational medium by which students give, receive, and seek feedback. How students perceive the feedback and how teachers communicate it is ultimately affected by different learner variables. These variables include self-esteem, agency, culture, and past experiences. They are influenced by the language we use and ultimately affected by the feedback shared within a classroom.

Self-Esteem

Giving and receiving feedback greatly affects self-esteem. How someone feels about learning cannot be separated from the act of learning itself; therefore, our strategies need to work to preserve students' self-esteem. Strategies that promote self-esteem include

- feedback framed in positive ways to ensure that as a class we are not causing harm to anyone
- strategies that focus on the task vs. the person
- explicitly taught language for use in conversations

Deliberate practice of our vocabulary, sentences, and questions are essential to ensure we are preserving self-worth and self-esteem, and are promoting learner agency and values. We need to pay close attention to the conversations among our students.

Agency

Learner agency is closely linked to personal choice, self-control, and autonomy within the classroom. The language we use while giving, receiving, and facilitating feedback is crucial to promoting learner agency in our students.

Culture

Feedback is the key to recognizing other cultures, experiences, norms, knowledges, and skills. Appropriate feedback that students feel safe enough to bring forth, along with feedback that students have learned to give and receive in appropriate ways, has the power to transform. The feedback evenly spreads the breadth of experiences and ideals within the classroom. Students can harness it to understand that what they do know and what they have experienced is important. They are all equally able to contribute to the classroom learning environment.

More than ever, multiple perspectives need to be celebrated. Cultural responsivity is essential in the classroom. The way that we give and receive feedback from one another is essential for learning about one another, developing self-esteem and tolerance in ourselves, among our peers, and in broader communities. We can implement feedback strategies that increase our understanding of diversity and how it affects academics, socialization, and development.

Talking Circles are a way that feedback-friendly classrooms can integrate feedback from members of the class; see page 44.

Past Experiences

Students bring their own personal experiences to the learning environment, and also need to engage in meaningful experiences to enhance the learning. Feedback with experiential learning is essential, helping to blend processes with content and to balance experience with content. For this to happen, safe spaces are needed to share experiences. Learning also needs to be personally relevant, so feedback and language also need to be personally relevant.

See Chapter 8 for more on the language of feedback.

Learning for the 21st Century

The feedback that attends to 21st-century skills can permeate the classroom and small-group discussions in multiple ways. We are accustomed to receiving feedback as written text and at certain end points in our learning; i.e., after a test or an essay. However, we can change our cognitive schema of feedback to view it as being incorporated into processes that occur throughout many interactions that take places within the classroom. We can infuse many more interactions with feedback in many ways, including the use of art, visualizations, drama, dance, role play, and other forms of discussion.

In classrooms, as in society, people are accountable to each other. Perhaps more important than knowledge itself is the way we communicate our knowledge and integrate new knowledge. We engage in strategies and processes to close the gaps between current learning behaviors and the goal behaviors. Feedback needs to be incorporated in ways that are meaningful for our students and learners. This is achieved by facilitating connections to 21st-century skills. Feedback can become a part of the conversations and discourse that happen in the classroom. Teachers are inevitably the facilitators of feedback interactions, so we can incorporate many different elements of student background, experience, previous knowledge, and multiple ways of knowing. Conversations can include listening, authenticity, and appropriately reaching out to one another.

See Chapters 4 to 7 for activities/strategies; see Chapter 8 for discussion of feedback-specific language.

The skills required in the feedback process are not just meaningful for the classroom, but also for new communities and new learning environments. Feedback for 21st-century skills incorporates aspects of socialization, academics, and development. The feedback processes also promote critical thinking, participatory learning, knowledge-building, problem-solving, inquiry, and collaborative networked learning—all skills that students will need to take with them into their futures.

It is often said that we have moved out of the Industrial Era into the Age of Knowledge, from a product economy to a knowledge economy. In a knowledge economy, students need to be able to think critically about new information. They need to assess how it fits in with what they already know. They also need to assess whether what they learn or know is "good" or valid information, and to be flexible in terms of changing their thinking when they learn new concepts. Even if students are not now part of a community that requires them to assimilate new information and accommodate their thinking to new communities and perspectives, they will be in the future. To be successful in working with knowledge, students need to be able to seek, ask for, and receive feedback appropriately. If feedback is linked to key 21st-century skills, it will help students achieve success within the Age of Knowledge. Problem-solving and critical thinking, collaboration, and being part of a global community are just a few of the crucial 21st-century skills we can build with our feedback.

Problem-Solving and Critical Thinking

What is new about the world we live in is not knowledge itself, but access to knowledge. Feedback can challenge us to solve problems in new ways because we acknowledge that students also have experiences and knowledge bases that affect learning. One strategy, for instance, involves questioning with feedback cards (see page 46). They can be used and internalized to help students self-motivate, motivate others to set new limits, expand their thinking, and solve problems in new ways. Sometimes we use technology as a tool to help students problem-solve. Problem-solving with technology in and of itself cannot convey to students how to find knowledge, discriminate between information sources, and build the new knowledge necessary for solving difficult problems. It is our feedback that serves as the currency that promotes problem-solving and critical thinking.

Collaboration

The most difficult task is to merge cooperation with collaboration.

Collaboration is somewhat different from cooperation. Cooperation refers to helping others who are working on similar goals. This is very common in classrooms: students all work toward the same learning goals at the same time. They can help each other and give and receive valuable feedback, but the focus for each is his/her work. Cooperation can be teacher-centred, with the teacher setting the tasks, the goals, and the ability of students to cooperate with each other.

Collaboration has quickly become an important skill in the 21st century. Collaboration refers to working together with others to drive learning forward, using shared goals and shared tasks. It is much more difficult to collaborate than to cooperate, due to power hierarchies and interpersonal conflicts. Collaboration is student-centred, with students taking responsibility for not only their own learning, but also for that of the group.

Globalization

Global interconnectedness is a reality of our world. Students and teachers alike will be called upon to collaborate and work toward shared goals and social issues. In our world, we need to know how to give and receive meaningful feedback with other people from other schools, other cities, and other countries. We need skill sets that help us to be open to cultural, racial, religious, and linguistic diversity. Developing technologies provide new opportunities for communication, the giving and receiving of feedback, to make productive changes.

There is a great deal of stress that goes along with rapid change. Responding to these changes in our schools and education can be helped with feedback. Feedback strategies help students and teachers to respond to current situations and to work for continuing changes.

Feedback extends across virtual, physical, and cultural domains. It is a model of collaboration that can extend across classrooms and libraries. The underlying philosophy of the feedback-friendly classroom encompasses the idea of all students working together in socially constructive ways. Feedback can also be used to help others learn effective cultural competencies in a globalized world. This feedback can then be a currency for building social, academic, and developmental capital, in our classrooms and beyond to global communities. Learning is contingent upon feedback, good or bad, and can play key roles in the interaction of individuals by pushing beyond the traditional curriculum and/or sum of existing ideas in the learning environment. It is not solely about the knowledge we build in the 21st century, but about the connections that we make between the ideas and knowledge. Global communities are a reality that will, and do, play a role in our learning. Therefore, we need feedback processes that promote excellent communication, learning, and connections.

> I understand the need to foster democracy to help my students harness quality feedback and use that learning to contribute to the improvement of society. For instance, in our current unit about the Regions of Canada, we are learning about unique environments and industries. We also see which animals have become endangered. As a class, we can decide on what we can do with this newfound knowledge to promote change to protect our endangered animals and preserve the natural environments within our regions of Canada. This is a humanistic endeavor as well, because it has the ability to help students become self-reflective about themselves and their own impact on the world, thus fostering happiness, aesthetics, spirituality, caring, and empathy (Ornstein, 2013, p. 41).

Information Technology

We are currently witnessing an explosion of edtech tools and technology for education purposes, including adaptive technology, interactive simulations, assessment technology, and tools for providing tutorials, information, collaboration, and more.

Learner-centred social interactions are essential to building and applying new knowledge. Web 2.0 technologies are powerful avenues for collaboration and integration. When feedback intermixes with other variables, new learning can occur. For instance, the design of the room, the relationships, the learning experiences, the student interests and goals all become necessary pieces of the puzzle for how students learn how to learn. Throughout their learning, students are invited to give and receive feedback, develop their approaches to their work, and transfer what they have learned to other learning. Feedback is a way to bring attention to new ideas, tools, spaces, questions, and information, and then to build and construct the learning. If we learn how to use feedback appropriately and successfully, students have the opportunity to drive their learning.

I believe that feedback is an emerging part of a pedagogy that fosters communication, collaboration, sharing, and use of technology in our connected world.

In keeping with the idea of the feedback-friendly classroom philosophy, edtech strategies can be harnessed using conversations, commenting, blogging, Tweeting, reflecting, and using talking circles and other key strategies to promote effective feedback. We can target excellent feedback strategies when we

- consider our own goals
- think about what we need to improve
- think about what we can say to improve ourselves, help someone else out, co-construct new knowledge
- figure out what strategies we can implement
- determine how it fits in with current subjects
- track and collect data that are meaningful to students, school, school community, global community, and assessment data

The Inquiry Process

A perpetual feedback process supports and enhances the process of inquiry. Inquiry involves, though is not limited to, students' ability to continue to ask questions and move their learning toward topics and knowledge they want or need to build next.

Feedback promotes inquiry; inquiry opens doors for feedback. It is a process that can continue to evolve. When we stifle the process of inquiry, we stifle the process of feedback. We want our students to ask questions and be able to take those questions through the processes that lead to answers. To do this, we need to teach students to stop regularly and seek feedback. *Do the other students understand your inquiry? Is the information that is being gathered in the process adequate? Does it keep you on the right track?* When students begin their inquiries and start with questions, they need help to hone them. Questioning is a skill; therefore, ample modeling, practice, and ongoing feedback are essential to ask appropriate questions.

Inquiry does not have to end after an assessment, nor does it have to be solely supported and driven by the teacher. Our mindsets can expand to include teaching students to become skilled at feedback processes.

Inquiry is much more complex than merely asking questions and finding answers. It is a process by which we encourage students to identify what they want or need to learn, to effectively find the best information they are seeking, and then to turn that information into something useful and continue with the inquiry process. Through inquiry, students keep personal control over their learning and proceed at their pace when they are ready for the next step. This enables them to ask the questions they need when they are personally ready for the answers, not when an educator deems it necessary for assessment. Asking questions and wondering about the world becomes normalized when we know that learning and feedback are always at work within the classroom. Even the end of a unit, a closed-inquiry process, or assessment with summative feedback are great opportunities to have students continue to interact with the feedback and allow their natural curiosities to drive new learning forward.

Collaborating with feedback is essential while engaging in inquiry. When students are given opportunities to share ideas and bounce them off each other, they exercise an inherent ability (sometimes with teacher guidance) to figure out with each other exactly where they need to be in their learning. What a great way to increase student agency! We not only should encourage students to share their ideas together and engage in peer assessment, but also should model the process of collaboratively refining their plans as they progress through their learning. As

Sharing is inevitably an important part of the learning process by which we gain feedback and give feedback to others.

See Chapter 8 for more on curriculum expectations and success criteria.

students work together to discover patterns and confirm or disprove hypotheses, we can help them clarify and extend their thinking. We can give them opportunities to demonstrate their understanding, skills, and knowledge in new ways.

When we allow students to share their learning in a safe environment, we provide opportunities for new ideas to develop and for fostering differentiated learning opportunities. Ongoing interactions with peers in collaborative situations are a powerful way for students to identify areas of strengths and limitations. It is important to integrate key information about strengths and weaknesses, interests and learning needs, to help students choose how they will represent their learning to others. Then we can feed this information forward to extend student learning to new contexts and learning opportunities, both inside and outside of the learning environment.

If we are conscious of the feedback that is already taking place, we can modify it to promote strong learning relationships and new levels of learning that extend much more deeply than the learning expectations. Self-feedback and peer feedback are essential to the feedback-friendly classroom as a natural process of students' development as learners. We can foster this process by setting up a classroom culture to support reflection and other key skills that promote growth and development. We can then flexibly assess student learning as it fits into the curriculum expectations and success criteria that we uniquely create together.

Designing Inquiry

To avoid problems with the uncontrolled and non-positive feedback students receive from their peers, with the dilemma of not getting around to each student, or with giving feedback too late within a task, we need to look at how we are designing our inquiry processes. We can break our learning processes into phases, with strategies to reinforce the feedback given to each student at each phase of the process. This is where we model feedback for our students and help them learn how to provide the right kind of feedback at each phase of the inquiry process. Further, we can provide opportunities to help students document and reflect on the feedback that they have received. Finally, they can incorporate this into their work throughout the process, before moving on to the next phase. The inquiry process involves four steps:

1. Acquire: Students acquire new information guided by learning goals, desired curriculum outcomes, and their questions. However, they do not always know if their questions are good questions. *Do other students understand what we are looking for with our questions? How can we find out?*
2. Manipulate: This is where students begin to build their plan for learning more information. The manipulation of information will be based on learning goals, previous knowledge, and future questions. This is where students start the process of building knowledge. *What do we do with this information? What technological tools are we using? What success criteria are we meeting? How do we manipulate the information to suit our academic purposes?* Note that manipulation is shaped by personal backgrounds, cultures, and experiences; it lies where teacher understanding meets the unique range of experiences brought forth by the students
3. Process: This stage deals with how our cognitive processes work to make meaning from the data we have acquired and manipulated. The information is processed via a strategy or organizational tool. *Did our information answer*

the questions we asked? Does it match the learning goals? How can we check this out and seek feedback before we present our findings?

4. Present: This final step is where students share with others, collaborate, and give and receive feedback about how the information relates to the learning goals and success criteria. Here is where new knowledge can emerge. Students can use the feedback they receive to make changes before they are given a final grade.

The Inquiry Process Circle

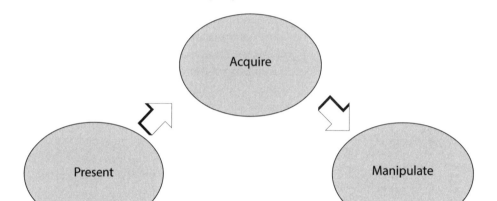

The Inquiry Process, the chart on page 25, can be used as a template for student questions, or as a guideline for working with the inquiry process. This chart can be photocopied, or scanned and uploaded for sharing on the interactive whiteboard. It can also be used by the teacher to keep notes of what is observed by the students. Making this chart available to students provides visual feedback for them. How a student or group of students answers the questions will provide them with valuable feedback. Further, it will provide the teacher with valuable information when conferencing with students.

The Inquiry Process

Step in the Inquiry Process	Asking Questions/ Seeking Feedback	Strategies for Eliciting Feedback	New Questions Generated by Students
Acquire	*What do I already know?* *What do I want to know?* *How can I find out?* *My idea is…* *How does it work?*	• Mind-mapping • Concept-mapping • Visualization • Verbal scaffolding	*Which questions do you like best?* *Do you have new questions?*
Manipulate	*What technological tools are we using?* *What success criteria are we meeting?* *How do we manipulate the information to suit our academic purposes?* *Where will I find the information?* *What knowledge-building strategies will be used?* *What do we do with the questions above?* *How will we research?*	Strategies depend on the repertoire that students have already learned or have available to them.	*What do we do with the questions above?* *How will we research?*
Process	*What does the new information mean to you?* *What do you need to know before you present your findings*	• Share work with the class on knowledge-building wall • Generate questions on sticky notes about the information being shared	*Were learning goals and success criteria met?*
Present	*What did I learn?* *What did I do well?*	• Feedback strategies; e.g., feedback cards	*What new questions do I now have?* *What would I do differently next time?*

Pembroke Publishers © 2015 *The Feedback-Friendly Classroom* by Deborah McCallum ISBN 978-1-55138-304-0

3

Designing Feedback Strategies

Creating a Theory of Action

Students become what they learn. As students embody knowledge, skills, and dispositions, they become the enhanced theories of their experiences. What this means is that they evolve into the learning that is happening for them through personal experience, knowledge-building, and, of course, feedback. Essentially, what students talk about and share with each other surrounding their experiences becomes their practice. To effectively design feedback strategies you can start with a theory of action, phrased as an *If...then...* statement. My theory became *If you become what you learn, then high-quality feedback you encounter and participate in will result in high-quality learning*. This high-quality learning will in turn result in a richer and more realistic theory of your own experiences.

My theory of action prompted me to consider the knowledge, skills, and dispositions that would need to be conveyed through feedback. I was then able to practice using different strategies to find which ones could take root, promote higher-quality feedback, and foster more realistic and deeper learning opportunities for my students.

Some questions for consideration when creating your own theory of action:

- Do we believe that we, as teachers, are the only ones to give feedback? Or do we allow students to recognize and learn how to effectively participate in the daily feedback experience?
- Do we allow students to develop feedback-giving and -receiving skills?
- Do we allow students' unique dispositions to come through in their feedback strategies?
- Are students allowed to develop their own theories of action, or are they limited to extensions of the teacher's theory of action?

We need to be aware that the strategies chosen will ultimately mean the omission of other strategies that students might find beneficial. Development of a theory of action should include the input of students, as they help co-develop feedback strategies. Use the Considerations When Designing Feedback Strategies template on page 34 to help you plan your feedback strategies.

Our students need help to learn how to effectively share nonevaluative feedback with each other. We need to provide them with an arsenal of explicit strategies

26

to ensure that we all can communicate appropriate and kind feedback with each other. As teachers, we begin our teaching with learning goals or essential questions for the students. We clearly communicate this by helping students visualize goals, and by providing checklists, rubrics, and other anchors for students to make meaningful connections between the learning goals and their future learning. Often, this happens at the beginning of a lesson or during our diagnostic assessments. However, we need to take this process further, to extend it from the before-learning stage to during-learning and after-learning stages. Instead of being teacher-driven, this kind of feedback will make students responsible for some of the feedback processes.

I have made use of many learning strategies throughout my career: Think–Pair–Share, graffiti, opinion lines, talking circles, values circles, and many, many more. But I had assessed these strategies through the lens of feedback as a principle, focusing on accountable talk, meeting or co-creating success criteria, minds-on learning, or brainstorming. My personal schemata for learning had not considered the use of these strategies specifically for promoting ongoing valuable communication patterns of feedback as a learning strategy. I came to realize that feedback is just as much a part of my learning as it is about the learning of others. A feedback-friendly classroom provides an overarching design, or a flexible framework, for respectful communication that drives learning forward. We can use feedback activities and strategies to help students understand just what they are required to do in terms of learning processes, but also to effectively help students to create and manage their own learning opportunities (Nuthall, 2007).

Consider a more traditional instructional design: the teacher provides students with the content and activities and then assesses their work; we assume that all students learn the same content in the same way; there are no guarantees that students will learn with feedback. It becomes clear that what we need to do is provide students with multiple feedback-friendly activities and strategies that allow them to interact with the content in socially appropriate ways. This can also serve to help move the learning and learning goals from short-term to long-term memory. A more feedback-friendly instructional design can help diminish misunderstandings that students may have, give students multiple opportunities to work with other students in the class and thus diminish the effects of power status, and provide more opportunities for teachers to work with students.

According to Brookhart (2011), effective feedback must

- be timely
- focus on one or more strengths and a next step
- focus on the process and not the student personally
- be descriptive, not judgmental
- be positive, clear, and specific

With these factors in mind, the success of the feedback-friendly classroom will be largely based on how we use our strategies that incorporate these elements.

Creating a Culture of Feedback

Giving and receiving feedback can be very difficult. Therefore, we need safe classroom cultures where all students can share emotions, thoughts, feelings, experiences, struggles, strengths, and questions. This involves the focus coming off the

Feedback-friendly activities help students shift their focus from themselves to the tasks at hand.

teacher as the "sage on the stage" and turning to the students to play active roles in feedback processes each day.

My favorite strategies have always included talking circles, restorative circles, and values circles. A circle is a sacred thing, with its roots in many First Nations cultures. In a circle, whoever is holding the talking feather, or other meaningful artifact, is the one gifted with the opportunity to talk. This is a great way to get to know others and share new ideas and feelings within the safety of the circle. What happens in the circle, stays in the circle—unless, of course, someone's safety happens to be at risk. Students are also respected with the right to pass. Values circles work to build self-esteem and build common language in giving positive feedback to another student. Prior classwork and brainstorming sessions, including practice sessions with other adults in the middle of the circle, are necessary to ensure success.

Building anchor charts with your class is a way to facilitate circles. The charts display key sentence starters, verbs, other vocabulary, feelings, and ideas of why something is important to the individual. This provides a concrete structure with key language that promotes positive and meaningful feedback. It also helps students move beyond more superficial forms of feedback, such as commenting on someone's new shoes, toward deeper aspects of what makes that person a good human being, what you learned from his/her ideas, etc. See page 35 for the Key Language for a Culture of Feedback template to help students brainstorm key language for building a safe feedback culture. Note that spaces are left to add your own language.

In creating a feedback-friendly culture, collaboration is essential. However, collaborating with others means allowing yourself to be vulnerable. The language we use can be harnessed to create a safe classroom. Therefore the language needs to be focused on the work, not the learner; it needs to encompass growth mindset; and it needs to follow the lead of the feedback that the learner gives him/herself. It also means putting the onus on the learner to take the lead. It is amazing how often students already understand what they did well and what they need to improve.

Feedback for Academics, Socialization, and Development

According to John Hattie, (Sutton, Hornsey, & Douglas, 2011), there are four distinct feedback levels:

1. Feedback related to the task.
2. Feedback related to the processes of learning: this type of feedback can lead to deeper learning.
3. Feedback related to self-regulation: metacognitive feedback that students seek and receive in productive ways.
4. Feedback related to the self: praise that very rarely leads to enhanced learning.

His levels of feedback prompted me to consider my three levels of feedback that I have associated with Academics, Socialization, and Development. Each of these is always focused more on the task or behavior, rather than the person. Also, each is enhanced with a focus on learning processes rather than products, and on self-regulation.

Students need to engage in feedback strategies as soon as possible after key learning. For instance, after students have the learning goals shared with them, they need to interact with them right away; after students have worked with a concept, immediate use of a strategy lets them interact with it in terms of explicit feedback.

Forget the feedback sandwich! In a feedback sandwich, negative feedback is cushioned with positive feedback. We don't want students to give each other any negative feedback. We want students themselves to be able to identify what they are doing well and what they need to improve on.

Specific strategies for feedback-friendly classrooms will be discussed in greater depth and detail in Chapters 4 through 7.

Further, feedback is always situated in the larger social context of the classroom. Each class is comprised of different learning needs, interests, cultures, knowledges, and experiences. It doesn't get any more authentic than the complex sets of interactions, interrelations, and connections that naturally occur within a classroom. The learning process is more than just the act of complying so that students can obtain the regurgitated knowledge from the teacher. The components of the classroom and learning come together to define the central core of what we need to succeed in the world.

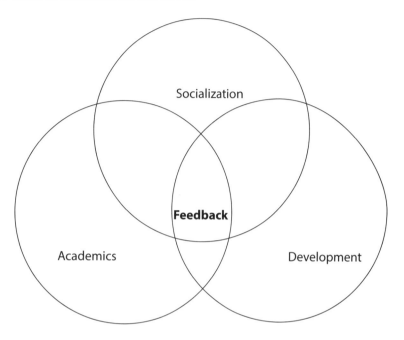

Academics

Feedback supports academics to help students learn *how* to think, not *what* to think. Feedback for academics includes giving and receiving feedback to determine not just what knowledge is the most important in the classroom, but also the best ways to acquire that knowledge. Academic-based feedback is used to actively construct the knowledge that we learn in prosocial ways. It involves the co-construction of learning goals and feedback strategies that build knowledge, understanding, and higher-order thinking processes. The kinds of academic skills that feedback can enhance include

- knowledge-building
- inquiry
- higher-order thinking
- subject-specific knowledge
- understanding
- communication
- application
- documentation
- observation
- questioning
- connecting
- reflection
- metacognition

In a feedback-friendly classroom, feedback about specific knowledge can emphasize any subject area; it can emphasize math, language arts, science, social studies, and other curricular areas. As a result, we can place a focus on the specialized vocabulary that goes with each subject area and include related inquiry processes. For example, if students are studying science, they would approach inquiry much like a scientist would; if they are studying social studies or history, they would approach inquiry from a lens of disciplinary thinking, like a social scientist or historian would. Therefore, feedback-friendly classrooms are structured to focus on the elements that are essential to different disciplines. In this way, feedback is used to enhance academics.

Socialization

Feedback for socialization includes the ability to ask appropriate and helpful questions and to engage in effective talk strategies. The teaching of such variables as language, vocabulary, and effective sentence starters needs to be explicit and deliberate at first, and then practiced until these variables become a part of the social fabric of the classroom. Strategies that recognize key differences across cultures and microcultures within the classroom are essential. Technology can be a valuable asset that allows for multiple ways of knowing to permeate the classroom and promote effective socialization skills. Strategies that promote socialization are also useful to feed forward information to support future learning. Socialization, therefore, becomes a natural part of the learning continuum from the start to the outcome, then to the next task. Supporting effective feedback for socialization does not mean we need to create more face-to-face interactions. While we may need to foster more social interactions, it is most likely the case that we need to work toward making the existing interactions of higher quality. We can do this with strategies that help students increase the quality of their socialization, that we will discuss in greater detail in Chapter 6: Feedback for Socialization.

Feedback that is learner-centred acknowledges that learning is not separate from the social lives that students lead. Feedback strategies that focus on the learning needs and interests of our students are organized to incorporate student lives and explicitly draw out the educational value of them. Strategies include opportunities to explore, to engage in inquiry and knowledge-building processes with others; for example, explicit questioning and talk circles. Questioning and other talk strategies also serve to help students recognize the differences across knowledge, experiences, and cultures within the classroom. Because we know that children's needs and interests cannot be pre-planned, we need an arsenal of strategies and feedback frameworks in place so we can meet needs and interests as they arise (Ornstein, 2013), so we can empower students to shape their learning within the contexts of learning goals, tasks, and strategies.

Development

When we consider strategies to support the feedback-friendly classroom, we also need to consider learner development. Of course, knowing what went well in the classroom is important, but this is not where we should just stop with the feedback process. This is where we need to step in with planning and prompts to help with the next stage of student development.

Feedback also needs to foster emotional and physical development. If it does not, then we risk fostering an academic hierarchy within the classroom. Teachers play an important role in shaping appropriate feedback for development within the classroom. This is especially true with younger students. We want feedback to adapt to the developmental level of the student, not the other way around. This is key because we are not training students for vocations, but educating students to become effective thinkers, with skills they will need throughout their lives. The kinds of skills that are emphasized in our feedback strategies include critical thinking, negotiation, flexible thinking, integrative thinking, analyzing information, finding the most salient information, and identifying next steps.

The levels that students will be able to engage in for meaningful feedback for learning will, in large part, depend on their maturity levels. However, even the youngest students can engage in certain ways.

Self-regulation is an important part of development. Social-emotional development is closely related to skills associated with academics and socialization. Self-regulation is a complex area of concern when it comes to our students because, according to Shanker (2013), self-regulation encompasses five domains: biological, emotional, cognitive, social, and prosocial. Though beyond the scope of this book to delve into each domain, Chapter 7: Feedback for Development will look more closely at feedback that can help us self-regulate as needed to help our students.

Three-Part Lesson Model

Feedback can be integrated throughout a three-part lesson that includes Minds-On, Action, and Consolidation. These three phases lead students through the feedback process through a gradual release of responsibility.

The next chapter will describe more strategies—many of them familiar. But they will be framed as part of a feedback-friendly process, such as a three-part lesson or gradual release model.

Minds-On

In this step you cognitively prepare students for thinking about the next feedback strategy they will be working with. It is critical that, before they use the strategy on their own, the strategy is modeled and students have the opportunity to think about it. You might even revisit learning that has taken place in a previous lesson, linking it to a particular feedback process. Some questions to ask include:

- What feedback form will students be working with?
- Is the feedback connected to the learning goals?
- Are you able to model the feedback first?

Action

In this phase, the students work individually or in small groups to solve a problem, answer a question, or engage in guided practice using feedback strategies. Students engage in strategies that might involve recording their thinking about the task in writing or orally, such as in a talking circle. The *action* here is not the lesson plan activities themselves; it instead refers to the feedback strategies that interweave the academics, socialization, or development being addressed in the lesson plan. Students can share their ideas; e.g., through a gallery walk. Whole-class discussion can ensue, and students can have opportunities to share constructive feedback and ask questions. Students are not just watching the feedback, or hearing about it; they are actively creating it. All students are sharing, learning from each other and about each other in safe ways, as a feedback-friendly classroom is being created.

Consolidation

Students are actively engaged with consolidating their learning through further self-reflection, summarizing their learning, and planning of next steps. Exit tickets are one strategy by which feedback can be shared as a way to do this. By this stage, students should be becoming more adept at using and sharing feedback, which will continue with the next three-part lesson.

Recording Feedback

There is no right or wrong way to record the learning and feedback taking place in the classroom. Every educator will have his/her personal feedback recording style to keep track of the data that supports assessment of the learning and feedback. Using various forms of organizers, you can start to see patterns of feedback and learning. By making these patterns visible, you can, in turn, gain more valuable information and feedback.

Shared with students without names attached, this information becomes a powerful social tool for learning. We all want to be seen as acceptable, and be accepted in our peer groups. This necessitates a safe learning environment in which we can explore our work safely and see the work of others. Then we can learn about new ways of thinking, validate our thinking, or change the way we think.

Learning Tracker

With a learning tracker, the teacher or student records the work or learning that was accomplished. The teacher can record key information from exit tickets about learning that went well and provide feedback to parents weekly, biweekly, or monthly. Students can use it to personally record key information to share at home. It is also reflective, in that it feeds back to the student, and transformative, in that it feeds forward to the teacher for the purposes of further instruction. This helps everyone get a better feel for the different ideas and perspectives within a classroom. The feedback processes in place help students shift attention away from the teacher and toward students' learning processes and responsibilities as learners. See page 36 for a Learning Tracker template.

Running Record

The running record is often used to assess student reading. However, we don't have widespread standardized prescribed assessments that benchmark where students should be socially or developmentally. Therefore, using a running record for feedback is different from the usual literacy running record. See page 37 for a Running Record template.

A feedback running record is based on your observations of students in terms of academics, socialization, or development. It is not necessarily about finding ways to calculate a final score or benchmark, but rather about gleaning information about patterns of learning.

Observations could include the following:

- Are students participating?
- Are students making meaning from their learning?

You can extract key information from feedback forms and post it in a newsletter to share with the class and parents. This helps everyone to get a better understanding of the different ideas and perspectives within a classroom.

- How close are students to the learning goals?
- Do students need prompts? What prompts will be effective?

A running record can be used to make notes of contributions during a talking circle. See page 44 for more on talking circles.

If you are ambitious, you can study the responses later and code them to find formal patterns or trends. More often than not, you will be able to see what feedback works, and what doesn't; which prompts work, and which don't.

A running record can also be used to assess how one student interacts with specific topics, line of inquiry, or learning goals. See page 37 for the Individual Running Record.

Weekly/Biweekly Report

Using the Weekly/Biweekly Report form on page 38 , you can make notes recording tasks that have been completed, tasks not completed, tasks that were done well, and next steps. This form goes home with students for parents to see. This is a great way to share basic information about each student's learning progress, and can form the basis of feedback between teacher, student, and home.

Considerations When Designing Feedback Strategies

Consideration	Checklist / Notes
Have you organized lessons and units around problems and student interests?	
Will subject matter be integrated across the curriculum?	
Do you plan to have students socially interact with the learning goals, big ideas, and success criteria?	
Are there regular opportunities to interact with accountable talk, goal-setting, and reflection on goals and learning processes?	
Is there a variety of instructional materials and resources available?	
Are plans available for whole-class, small-group, and individualized work?	
Is it possible to make scheduling flexible, with adjustable time periods to promote the talk that creates a feedback-friendly classroom?	
Are you open to flexible and changeable groupings?	
What strategies for differentiating do you have?	
Will students have active opportunities to seek information that they can use?	
How will you facilitate a variety of classroom experiences and instructional situations?	
How will you promote equal, yet flexible, standards, with consideration for different levels of achievement?	

Adapted from Ornstein (2013).

Pembroke Publishers © 2015 *The Feedback-Friendly Classroom* by Deborah McCallum ISBN 978-1-55138-304-0

Key Language for a Culture of Feedback

Sentence Starters	*Thank you for…* *What I liked about… was…* *What I appreciated was …* *You affected me when…* *I felt…* *The light bulb went on for me when…* *You showed integrity when…*	Add your own
Words of Appreciation	*gracious* *helpful* *selfless* *kind* *friendly* *cooperative* *honest* *collaborative* *inclusive* *patient* *empathetic*	Add your own
Verbs	*learning* *reading* *cooperating* *collaborating* *talking* *playing* *helping* *demonstrating* *showing* *waiting* *leading* *participating*	Add your own
Feelings	*happy* *sad* *glad* *relieved* *inspired* *shocked* *confused* *helpless* *friendly*	Add your own

Pembroke Publishers © 2015 *The Feedback-Friendly Classroom* by Deborah McCallum ISBN 978-1-55138-304-0

Learning Tracker

Week #	What I accomplished	What I learned	Next Steps
Math			
French			
Language Arts			
Social Studies			
Science			

Pembroke Publishers © 2015 *The Feedback-Friendly Classroom* by Deborah McCallum ISBN 978-1-55138-304-0

Running Record

Name	Observations

Individual Running Record

Name: _____

Topic/Line of Inquiry	Observations

Weekly/Biweekly Report

Name: _____

Weekly/ Biweekly (circle one)	Math	Language	Art	Science	Social Studies	Other
Tasks Completed and Notes						
Incomplete Tasks and Notes						
Next Steps						

Pembroke Publishers © 2015 *The Feedback-Friendly Classroom* by Deborah McCallum ISBN 978-1-55138-304-0

4

Feedback Strategies

Each of the strategies presented can be used to support any or all of Academics, Socialization, and Development.

Teachers are ultimately the ones responsible for ensuring student learning. We can help our students by giving them ample opportunity to give, receive, and seek feedback over time. The first thing we do is engage in deliberate planning for our students. We create our lesson and unit plans to provide the frameworks for organizing our time with the students, and deliberately set out the strategies we will use to help them give, receive, and seek feedback.

Teacher guidance is always necessary to help students approach their learning in the best ways possible. Careful planning of feedback strategies is essential. The strategies we use should have the ability to nurture the individual and developmental growth of each student. Selecting the language, routines, objects for learning, and opportunities for sharing content must happen in developmentally appropriate ways, while following the frameworks of our curriculum documents. We know that classroom environments influence the quality of student learning. We also know that many of the same topics and big ideas are taught from grade to grade, with increasing complexity and at higher levels of difficulty. We can use feedback as diagnostic tools to understand where our students are.

The range of strategies presented in this chapter is by no means exhaustive. Many activities and strategies already in use in your classroom represent valuable means of eliciting, giving, and supporting feedback: e.g., drawing a picture, role-play, student graffiti, KWL, journaling, reflective journal, blogging.

In a feedback-friendly classroom, we want to build more meaningful connections and relationships to facilitate better sharing of feedback. Traditionally, the teacher disseminates the feedback and gives it to the students; the teacher has control. The feedback-friendly classroom is not about handing control over to the students; it is about using strategies and redesigning the ways that interactions become shared in the classroom. It is about transferring more responsibility for learning to the students. Feedback strategies can help unlock the creative potential of students in both their learning of content and personal development.

Meta-Feedback

This strategy helps to support metacognition within the classroom for the purposes of giving feedback. Meta-feedback is based on the literacy strategy of making connections: students make connections of self-to-text, self-to-self, or self-to-world. Using meta-feedback, students

- give feedback relating to the content they are studying

- give feedback to themselves on their learning
- give feedback on how the learning relates to the world

Meta-feedback supports connections between subjects, learning goals, and success criteria. Students also learn how to recap and summarize their learning, or make necessary changes in reiteration of their goals.

To encourage this strategy, you require space and time to facilitate meaningful conversations. Sometimes this means being flexible with schedules to allow for this kind of dialogue and reflection to take place. It is sometimes impossible, but if the meta-feedback strategy is made a priority, you can leverage the benefits of creating a feedback-*friendlier* classroom than the one you currently have.

Use the Meta-Feedback template on page 52 to cue students to focus on meta-feedback or to record their feedback. Note that the template can be used for a whole-class activity if posted on the interactive whiteboard or chart paper.

Success Criteria

Success criteria can be embedded within a variety of strategies to help students make meaningful connections with learning goals. After co-creating success criteria with students, you can return to them with continual discussion and negotiation of learning tasks, while keeping the main ideas and learning goals intact. Establishment of success criteria is essential to feedback on each other's work. It is an excellent anchoring mechanism to the learning on hand. Success criteria cue the knowledge and skills that students need to keep coming back to within their interactions in the classroom.

On page 53 is a simple Success Criteria Checklist that can be used to keep track of success criteria and if they have been met. Students can use it by checking off if they think they achieved the success criteria. They can also use the checklist with their peers. The Comments or Observations section can be used by the teacher as a lead-up to the final reflection section.

Entry and Exit Tickets

Learners feel more motivated when they have opportunities to experience autonomy, to have feelings of competence, and to relate to one another (Ryan & Deci, 2000). Therefore, learning strategies to promote active and volitional learning, as opposed to passive and controlled learning, will provide different kinds of feedback and propel learning forward (Ryan & Deci, 2000, p. 55).

Entry tickets can set the stage for giving feedback by eliciting information about how a student is feeling about previous knowledge and learning.

Sample Entry Ticket

Question	Response
How are you feeling today?	
What do I already know about this?	
What do you remember from yesterday's lesson?	
What does this mean to you?	

The feedback gleaned from an exit ticket can be coded to highlight key variables, including positive, negative, and neutral comments; questions and concerns; requests and suggestions; comments on materials and activities; and information relating to other students (Hayes, 2008). The feedback can be harnessed to pinpoint strengths, interests, questions and gaps in learning, and also to gain information about learning strategies being used, including literacy strategies and learning skills.

Information from exit tickets can be compiled within a spreadsheet to find patterns. One way to do this is to create an online form from the exit ticket questions, with student responses being automatically placed in a spreadsheet. This allows you to see the patterns and trends that arise. You can use this information to analyze vocabulary, accountable talk, and learning gaps and strengths. It can help you further adapt instruction.

Sample Goal-Setting Exit Ticket

Question	Response
What are your learning goals?	
What have you done to achieve your goals?	
What will you do this term to achieve your goals?	

Sample Reflection Exit Ticket

What I liked:	
What I didn't like:	
What I want to do:	

Exit tickets can be turned into free-writing activities and put in an e-portfolio or a blog post. What an excellent way for students, teachers, and parents to monitor their own personal feedback over time! Regardless of how you use the information from an exit ticket, it can help you and your class customize your feedback-friendly culture.

Gallery Walk

In this activity, student work is displayed visually around the classroom. Students have the opportunity to walk through, as they would in a formal art gallery. This popular strategy is well-suited to the purpose of thinking about and sharing feedback. Students can use sticky notes attached to the work to ask questions of the creator of the work. Positive comments about the work are also welcomed, once students have had a chance to co-create appropriate language. It is important to meet as a class after the gallery walk to discuss thoughts and impressions and have students share questions that they can answer, thus giving and receiving meaningful feedback. By using sticky notes for questions and feedback, this stage can be completely anonymous, ensuring the safety of the feedback process. A gallery walk helps students make new connections, learn from others, and have an opportunity to change their final product before handing in a task for more formal assessment.

Mind-Mapping

Each student can use a personal color in the mind map; this allows you and students to analyze the colors and see where gaps in knowledge may need to be filled in.

Mind-mapping is a way to make learning visible and provide valuable feedback to the teacher. In a mind-map, learners can connect ideas, view and analyze different points of view, identify strengths, and form new ideas. It can be used for much more than just brainstorming. Mind-mapping encourages students to make physical representations of their thinking. It is effective in generating feedback on what the group already knows and where they need to go next. Group mind-mapping takes the pressure off individual students by looking at the collective knowledge of the group. Clear connections to existing knowledge and learning goals can be made.

- A great first step before mind-mapping is to agree on keywords. When keywords are co-constructed and agreed upon by teachers and students, communication can be enhanced and confusion minimized.
- Lines can be drawn in different colors to connect ideas. For instance, there could be lines for distracting thoughts; this allows students to recognize their thoughts as being relevant or not. Connecting thoughts can open the doors for new lines of thought. Or you can specify lines for questions and wonderings, and lines for what is missing.

See page 54 for a Mind Map template.

When we validate the thinking of others and our own thinking, we also help students build self-esteem and understand the value they bring to the classroom. This further builds in opportunities for metacognition, which, as we know, provides more rich information and feedback into student thinking.

Artifacts

Artifacts can work as anchors, cueing mechanisms, visual connections, and reminders of the learning that is happening within the classroom learning environment. They help students visualize; this is a powerful comprehension strategy. If students can learn to use artifacts to make connections when they are giving, receiving, and seeking feedback, their comprehension of the feedback itself will be greatly enhanced. For instance, students could make a 3D artifact that represents a character or object, and then speak/write to that object and describe how it is connected to the learning goals.

Talking Circles

In a talking circle, we speak and listen to understand. Circles are significant to many First Nations, Metis, and Inuit cultures. They are interconnected, representing continuity and ever-evolving knowledge. This interconnectedness is a key component of a feedback-friendly classroom.

Talking circles are also an excellent way to help students make connections to feedback, including verbal scaffolding.

In a talking circle, students have opportunities to share the experiences, knowledge, vocabulary, language, and values that are significant to them. The talking-circle paradigm can become embedded in classroom goals, criteria, rules, and overall management framework. The language used in talking circles is inclusive and shared throughout the class, becoming unique to the class and evolving through everyone's contributions. Such a language demonstrates respect. Talking circles can become the foundation of the feedback that is appropriate for that particular classroom.

You can record participation in a talking circle using the Talking Circle template on page 55. Write the initials of each student to mark where they are sitting. Mark with an X or check mark every time someone speaks; you can annotate each incidence of circle talk. This can serve as a form of pedagogical documentation that gives valuable information about who is most comfortable and confident in giving feedback.

Think–Pair–Feedback

Remind students that the focus should be on tasks, topics, ideas, and questions—not on persons.

Think–Pair–Feedback activities are beneficial for a feedback-friendly classroom because they allow students to stop and think about the topic before they share feedback with a partner. When a student is afforded the time to stop and think, it allows the student space and prevents impulsivity. Students can be gently directed to anchor charts, including success criteria, learning goals, and the explicit language and ideas of giving and receiving feedback.

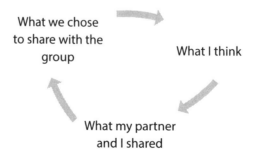

What we chose to share with the group

What I think

What my partner and I shared

Options for recording Think–Pair–Feedback information include students recording their thoughts on the Think–Pair–Feedback template on page 56, the teacher recording students' thoughts in an anchor chart, and students sharing their thoughts orally or on a blog (see page 57 for a Think–Pair–Blog organizer).

Learning Contract

A learning contract is a good way to teach and support the feedback process. Having students sign a learning contract helps them commit to their responsibilities to a feedback-friendly classroom, and lets them know that it will be a safe place for them to give and receive feedback. See page 58 for a Learning Contract template.

Co-create the learning contract with your class. Student responsibilities could look like this:

- To put forth best effort
- To demonstrate a growth mindset
- To make mistakes and learn from them
- To focus on the process
- To understand that learning is hard
- To give and receive feedback in appropriate ways
- To promote a feedback-friendly classroom

Teacher responsibilities should show that you are bound by the same feedback process and criteria as students, but with added responsibility for moving learning forward:

- To demonstrate a growth mindset
- To focus on the process
- To understand that learning is hard
- To give and receive feedback in appropriate ways
- To promote a feedback-friendly classroom
- To give and receive feedback and adapt instruction accordingly

Stop/Start/Continue

Stop/Start/Continue can also act as a form of self-feedback if you are looking to help students reflect and think more deeply about their unique roles and contributions to the learning process.

This activity can help the class reflect on feedback processes at work in the classroom. It elicits student feedback on routines and situations that students feel uncomfortable with, or think are not helpful; ideas for practices that could be initiated to improve how the class operates; classroom patterns that they are happy with and want to continue. You can use the Stop/Start/Continue template on page 59 to record the feedback the students share.

Strategies that Combine Positive Feedback and Next Steps

Plus/Idea/Next Step

Using the Plus/Idea/Next Step chart on page 60, students share a positive comment or observation, a new idea, and a next step or new question. It has a wide variety of applications, including establishing success criteria, sharing feedback between students, eliciting feedback from students, and student self-evaluation.

Instead of including a Minus column, which necessitates negative feedback, this strategy gives students permission to offer a suggestion based on what they have already learned. It is a collaborative and culturally responsive way to acknowledge the importance of knowledge coming from a student's own personal experiences and cultural background.

Two Stars and a Wish

Similar to the Plus/Idea/Next Step strategy, Two Stars and a Wish allows students to provide positive feedback and to consider moving the learning forward. In the feedback-friendly classroom, the use of this popular strategy should always be anchored to the learning goals. It helps students focus on positive aspects of the learning and think about next steps. Whether students write this information or share it orally in a conference, it helps the giver of feedback to keep coming back to the learning goals. See page 61 for templates to copy and distribute.

One to Glow, One to Grow

Here is another, slightly different, approach to how conversation and ideas can be molded around learning goals. Students give one to glow (a positive comment), and one to grow (an idea or suggestion for improvement), and the emphasis remains on the fact that we all can grow by considering the ideas of others.

Feedback Footprint

You can choose to have students record their feedback footprint in a form that would allow them to reflect on the growth of their feedback skills; see Feedback Footprint Organizer on page 63.

This strategy is a way for students to informally record their own impact on learning throughout the school year/term. Students can create a Foot-Folio, a feedback footprint and portfolio in one. They collect examples of how they affected someone positively with feedback. The goal is that at the end of the term each student will have an extensive Foot-folio that demonstrates their acquisition and use of feedback skills, including the ability to interact positively, to ask meaningful questions, to contribute ideas, and to help create a safe and feedback-friendly classroom. See page 62 for a template for a Foot-folio.

Feedback Cards

Feedback Cards are a way to anchor student learning to specific areas of feedback. They use written and/or visual cues to help students organize their thinking about learning: cues can include strategies, questions/prompts, sentence starters, language, etc. They actively and holistically involve students in the feedback process; they allow students to be teachers, and teachers to learn alongside their students.

You can use Feedback Cards to guide the entire feedback process in your classroom. Use of them makes feedback visible, reinforces feedback-friendly language and accountable talk, promotes growth mindsets, and enhances essential socialization, academics, and student development. Feedback Cards are also effective in helping students practice the language they use in giving and receiving feedback. There are no wrong answers. They can be used as a form of self-assessment, or as feedback-friendly assessment—not evaluating another person's work, but using the prompts to practice focusing on particular aspects of someone's work.

Feedback Cards can be printed and laminated, used with magnets on whiteboards, or posted on walls, chart paper, bulletin boards, desks, and floors. They can be organized in various formations, including matrices, graphs, mind maps, or life-size rubrics. They can be annotated with sticky notes, or you can use the templates provided in this book to record thinking and extensions. When made visible, feedback can be captured for websites, blogs, and e-portfolios, or used as a visible anchor for the learning happening in the subject, lesson/unit, etc. A different card could also be created and printed for any curriculum goal or expectation; you can create your own deck for each subject.

You can use recipe cards or rectangles of any card stock. Or see page 64 for blank Feedback Card forms that can be photocopied or printed out and laminated.

Feedback Cards to Elicit Feedback

Each card represents a feedback strategy, with a simple graphic on the front side of the card and instructions on the back. The cards can be used as cues to help students decide how to discuss a problem or start thinking about a topic. You can construct a feedback card for each strategy, including, but not limited to, the following

Entry and Exit Tickets	Gallery Walk	Mind-Mapping
Artifacts	Talking Circles	Think–Pair–Feedback
Stop/Start/Continue	Plus/Personal Idea/Next Step	Two Stars and a Wish
One to Glow, One to Grow	Role-Play	Graffiti

Sample Feedback Cards: Feedback Strategies —Front

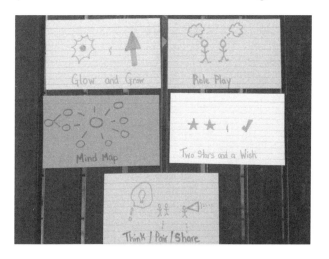

Sample Feedback Cards: Feedback Strategies —Back

Feedback Cards to Share Feedback

A simple set of three Feedback Cards can help students describe how they share feedback, receive feedback, and seek feedback and evaluate the feedback they receive. They provide the basis of your own personal set of Feedback Cards.

Share	Receive	Seek/Evaluate

Students can use Feedback Cards assigned or chosen as prompts, and then can share their feedback orally, visually, or in text. Any of the templates in this book can be used to record student answers, either by writing or on sticky notes placed in the appropriate columns. The real work comes from students filling out their sticky notes and templates, making drawings, etc., to describe how they share, receive, seek and evaluate feedback they are given.

Feedback Cards as Checklists

See the chapters on Feedback for Academics, Feedback for Socialization, and Feedback for Development for more on use of Feedback Cards.

Feedback Cards can be printed out, laminated, and used as cues; they can be placed on word walls or can become headings for checklists for observing and assessing students. Just a few of the many ideas for using Feedback Cards to organize learning:

Learning Goals	Personal Goals	Success Criteria
Academic Learning	Socialization	Development

Feedback Cards for Adapting Criteria

Teacher and students can use Feedback Cards to make visible adaptations to the success criteria for their own needs. This is a process that can help students learn to individualize and recognize how adaptations can be made, recognize the needs of others, and keep their own needs and those of others in mind when providing feedback. It also reminds all students that the same high standards are still permeating the classroom.

Feedback Dice

Feedback Dice can be beneficial for primary or students who appreciate having tasks/strategies or prompts chosen for them.

The goal of student-centred Feedback Dice is to increase the confidence of students. They help us understand more about how the students think and what is most meaningful for them. With Feedback Dice, we can go much deeper than basic brainstorming to learn about the students. We then can use what we learn about our students to shape our practice. We need to be flexible enough to change our strategies to be able to meet the students where they are at, not just where we want them to be, or where they feel pressured to be. Feedback Dice can be used by individuals, in pairs, or in small groups. They can be used with any subject and can be integrated with social or developmental aspects of learning.

The Feedback Dice prompts can be put on Feedback Cards. However, dice are a fun way for some students to randomly roll the prompts they will use.

A set of six Feedback Dice create a toolkit for using feedback in the classroom. Each die has a text cue and a visual to help students make connections:

Die 1: Prompt
Die 2: Appreciation
Die 3: Task
Die 4: Question Word
Die 5: Next Word
Die 6: Form of Feedback

See page 65 for a template for creating your own dice.

Teachers or students can decide how many dice to use. For instance, two dice—a Prompt die and an Appreciation die—can be rolled to prompt learning associated with socialization. A Question die and a Next Word die can be rolled together to help students with inquiry. Or a die could be used to help students figure out how they will share their learning.

Feedback Dice can be a tool to prompt feedback for academics, socialization, or development. They can also focus on 21st-century skills, including collaboration, inquiry, problem-solving, global connections, and cultural responsiveness.

Die 1: Feedback Prompts

Write one prompt on each side of the die. Note that prompts can focus on Academics, Socialization, or Development.

Sample Academic Prompts

- How do you know that?
- *I agree with _____ because…*
- *I disagree because…*
- *This reminds me of…*
- *I figured out that…*
- Say more about that.
- Give an example.
- *What I learned was…*
- Repeat what was just said.
- Elaborate.
- Explain your strategy.
- What do you still want to know?
- Ask your own question.
- Share anything you want to share.

Sample Development Prompts

- What went well?
- What did not go well?

- *I am good at...*
- *I am proud of...*
- *I don't understand about...*
- *I understand that...*
- *To improve, I need to...*
- *Next time this happens I will...*
- What are your goals?
- What do you need clarified?
- Ask your own question.
- Share anything you want to share.

Sample Socialization Prompts

- *I can take care of myself by...*
- *I feel best when...*
- *I feel terrible when...*
- How do you tell a joke?
- What is your favorite character trait?
- How do you know if someone is a friend?
- What are the traits of a good friend?
- How do you encourage someone else?
- What helps you feel encouraged to do your best?
- What is peer pressure?
- What behavior is acceptable in _____ situation?
- Help us understand.
- What facial expressions show interest?
- How does your body language show interest?
- Ask your own question.
- Share anything you want to share.

Die 2: Appreciation Prompts

Write one way of showing appreciation on each side of the die. The following are adjectives and words of appreciation that can apply to academics, socialization, or development. They work particularly well for value circles!

- *Thank you for...*
- *You were thoughtful when...*
- *You were generous when...*
- *You were helpful when...*
- *I appreciated it when...*
- *I learned from you that...*

Die 3: Tasks

Write one task on each side of the die. These learning strategies are particularly helpful for students to explore feedback for Academics.

- Observe
- Notice
- Remember
- Identify
- Compare

- Contrast
- Visualize
- Describe
- Predict
- Explain
- Retell
- Infer
- Underline
- Highlight
- Reflect
- Relate
- Connect
- Main Idea
- Find

Die 4: Question Words

Write one question word on each side of the die. Question words will be rolled out to find out which question the student will ask.

- Who
- What
- When
- Where
- Why
- How

Die 5: Next Words

Write one next word on each side of the die. When rolled with the Question Word die, this die shows where the question is going.

- Is
- Can
- Should
- Could
- Would
- Will
- Might
- Did

Die 6: Ways of Sharing Feedback

The Feedback Dice Form on page 66 can be used by students to record personal thinking or by the teacher to keep track of who is sharing.

Write one form of feedback on each side of the die.

- Verbal Face-to-Face
- Written
- Audio
- Video
- Picture with Explanation
- Conference with Teacher and Peer

Meta-Feedback

Name: _____

Subject: _____

Activity: _____

Feedback-to-text	Feedback-to-self	Feedback-to-world

Success Criteria Checklist

Name: _____

Subject: _____

Lesson or Goal: _____

Success Criteria	Met/Not Met	Comments or Observations
1.		
2.		
3.		
4.		
5.		
6.		

Reflection

Mind Map

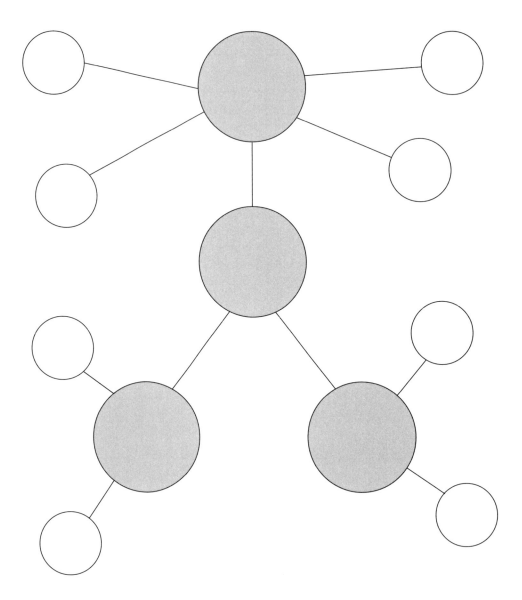

Reflection

Based on our mind-mapping strategy, this is what I/we already know:

I think I am/we are still missing

This is what I/we will do next:

Pembroke Publishers © 2015 *The Feedback-Friendly Classroom* by Deborah McCallum ISBN 978-1-55138-304-0

Talking Circle

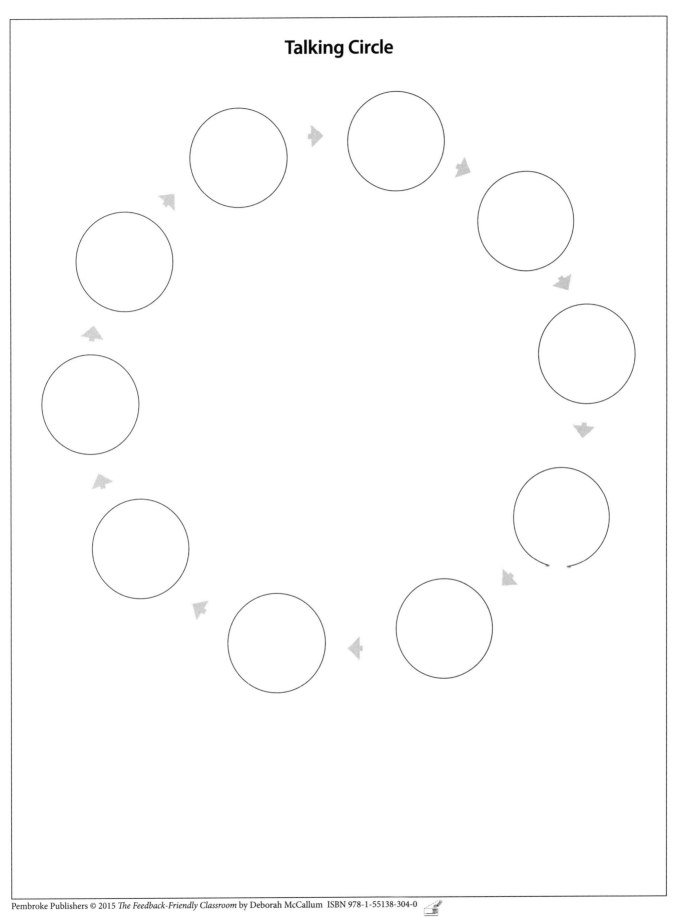

Think–Pair–Feedback

Think	Pair	Feedback

Pembroke Publishers © 2015 *The Feedback-Friendly Classroom* by Deborah McCallum ISBN 978-1-55138-304-0

Think–Pair–Blog

The idea I shared

My partner's idea that stood out most for me

What I learned

What I missed

What I do next

Pembroke Publishers © 2015 *The Feedback-Friendly Classroom* by Deborah McCallum ISBN 978-1-55138-304-0

Learning Contract

Teacher/Class: _____   Student: _____

Learning Goals:

Student's Responsibilities:

Teacher's Responsibilities:

_____   _____
Student Signature   Teacher Signature

Pembroke Publishers © 2015 *The Feedback-Friendly Classroom* by Deborah McCallum ISBN 978-1-55138-304-0

Stop/Start/Continue

Stop	Is there anything that we as a class should stop doing? Why?
Start	Is there anything as a class that we should start doing? Why?
Continue	Is there anything as a class that we should continue? Why?

Plus/Idea/Next Step

Feedback on _____	+ Share a Plus (something positive about the task or behavior)	Idea What new idea(s) would you add from your personal experience, culture, and knowledge?	Next Step What is the next step? Do you have a new question?

Two Stars and a Wish

Star	
Star	
Wish	

Star	
Star	
Wish	

Pembroke Publishers © 2015 *The Feedback-Friendly Classroom* by Deborah McCallum ISBN 978-1-55138-304-0

Foot-Folio Template

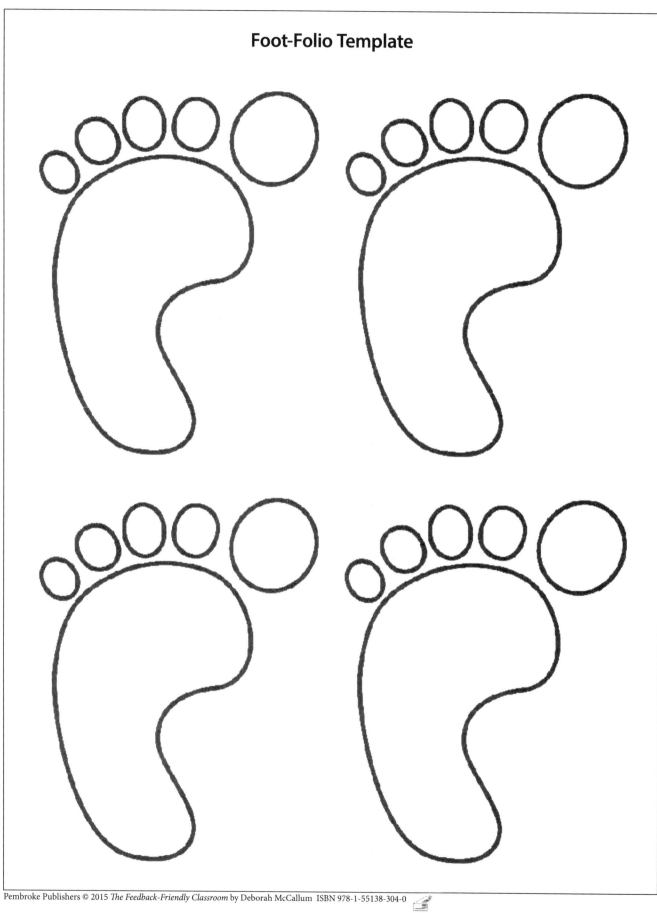

Feedback Footprint Organizer

Date	Positive impact you had on someone	Anything you would do differently next time?

Pembroke Publishers © 2015 *The Feedback-Friendly Classroom* by Deborah McCallum ISBN 978-1-55138-304-0

Feedback Card Template

Pembroke Publishers © 2015 *The Feedback-Friendly Classroom* by Deborah McCallum ISBN 978-1-55138-304-0

Feedback Dice Template

Feedback Dice Form

Student Name	Prompt	Appreciation	Task/ Learning Strategy	Question Word	Next Word	Form of Feedback

5

Feedback for Academics

You can use the Strategies for 21st-Century Skills Checklist on page 74 to plan the feedback strategies according to the skills of collaboration, inquiry, problem-solving, global connections, and cultural responsiveness.

In any classroom, feedback for assessment and for learning is most obvious as a way of feeding into curriculum learning and academic achievement. Most strategies are conventionally used in this capacity, and all of the strategies explored in Chapter 4 are no different. This chart shows how different feedback strategies can be used for stages of any lesson.

Feedback Strategies for Lesson Stages

Minds-On
- Learning Contract (page 45)
- Talking Circle (page 44)
- Entry Tickets (page 41)

Brainstorm
- Mind-Mapping (page 43)
- KWL
- Graffiti
- Graphic Organizers
- Sticky Notes

Group Work
- Think–Pair–Feedback (page 44)
- Feedback Cards (page 46)
- Feedback Dice (page 49)
- Two Stars and a Wish (page 46)
- One to Glow, One to Grow (page 46)
- Plus/Idea/Next Step (page 46)
- Start/Stop/Continue (page 45)

Scaffolding
- Next Steps
- Reflection Journal
- Weekly/Biweekly Report (page 33)

Reflection
- Journal
- Feedback Footprint (page 46)
- Blogging
- Draw a Picture
- Exit Tickets (page 41)

Feedback Strategies for Comprehension

The literacy benefits of practicing feedback include creating deeper understandings of what students read; verbalizing thinking; applying vocabulary and sentence starters; and providing opportunities for self- and peer-feedback. These are very important for creating a culture of learning together through the art of feedback.

Key comprehension strategies that we may see in our literacy curricula can also be modified and applied to feedback processes. For instance, the meta-feedback strategies of feedback-to-self, feedback-to-text, and feedback-to-world (see page 40) are part of the connecting processes for improving academics with feedback.

The way we organize our language will significantly affect these tasks. Therefore, it is important to pre-determine the key vocabulary needed for each lesson or unit. This can be accomplished by using word-vocabulary templates, graphic organizers, and word walls. Talking circles can be used as a collaborative strategy to elicit the kind of vocabulary and language for feedback from students that is meaningful to them. Feedback Dice or Feedback Cards elicit vocabulary and sentence starters that can be shared on a bulletin board display or in another visual way. This strategy can be used with individual students, together as a class using chart paper and sticky notes or as an online document, or on pieces of chart paper for a small-group exercise.

Cultural responsiveness is another key component of feedback strategies for comprehension; it allows us to better understand and make connections, predictions, visualizations, and inferences.

Feedback cues, both verbal and nonverbal, can help students make deeper connections to the texts they are working with in class, whether they are visual, mathematical, or literary. Feedback facilitates deeper learning and a greater ability to engage in problem-solving and transfer essential skills into other facets of life, including family, environmental issues, school, pets, community, and globalization.

Feedback Activities for Connecting

After students have worked on an academic activity—e.g., reading a passage, researching, or completing a writing exercise—it is important to use feedback to help them make connections surrounding their academic work.

To make connections between academic learning and feedback to share, students can also use a Venn diagram. With a Venn, a student can compare two different texts or other work products. Out of their brainstorming, students can use a Venn diagram to demonstrate their meta-feedback: feedback-to-text; feedback-to-self; feedback-to-world.

Sample Venn Diagram

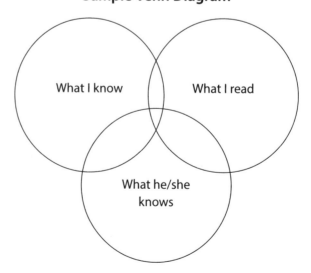

What I know

What I read

What he/she knows

Meta-feedback Questions

Any learning that is shared can help students generate feedback about the task and learning itself. This is crucial for students if they are giving feedback to others as well, because if they are involved with peer feedback, they must focus on the task and not the person.

Feedback-to-text questions might include

What was this task about?
What did you understand?
What do you still have questions about?
What was the most confusing part of this activity/learning?

Feedback-to-self questions can be asked as part of a Think–Pair–Feedback, a mind map, a talking circle, or an exit ticket. They can help students think about themselves and their own lives in relation to their learning:

What does this learning remind you of?
What experiences in your own life connect to this piece?
Do you have any other personal connections?

Feedback-to-world questions can help students make connections between their learning and the larger or global community:

What is the world issue that this learning could relate to?
Does it remind you of a situation you have seen or heard of in your life?
How does it relate to the greater/global community?

Feedback Activities for Visualizing

It is no secret that visualization is an important part of comprehension in learning. Visual-based feedback gives students the opportunity to apply feedback strategies in text-free ways. It is important to remember that students need plenty of time to practice giving and receiving feedback. It takes time to use feedback to help make deeper connections. Students need a lot of guidance.

- Feedback Dice and Cards can be used to provide visual cues. The anchor charts, word walls, portfolios, and templates created by strategies in Chapter 4 also provide visual cues for giving and receiving effective feedback. Here, feedback supports a deeper understanding of the academic content. The visuals serve as cues that can help students to retrieve what they already have learned about giving and receiving feedback, and to better apply it to the academic content.
- Through the strategies in Chapter 4, students learn to give feedback in ways that makes their thinking visual. For instance, during meta-feedback, students can be asked to develop pictures in their minds and describe them. Students can be asked to create pictures after interacting with the academic content while other students can be creating visualizations of the feedback they received. Feedback strategies help to scaffold the learning to the next level and this can be done visually. Instead of writing each new step in the learning process, a picture or icon can be created by students to help them

There are useful programs on the Internet with visuals that can be used on Feedback Cards as cues for learning; for example, Pixabay.com provides images free for commercial use.

understand and "see" what their next step will need to be. Students can visualize by creating illustrations that depict the imagery they have in their minds while listening/processing an idea, presentation, story, answer, etc.

- When students can practice visualization, it helps to make the academic learning more engaging. It makes it personal, promotes shifts in thinking, elicits memories and feelings, and adds dimensions to learning that promote retrieval of information. As a result, the feedback becomes much more dynamic.
- The use of artifacts is another strategy that increases learning, engagement, and feedback. Choose a significant tool, idea, or item that best represents something important about the academic content.
- Imaged-based feedback can be done in smaller pieces; e.g., as part of the scaffolding process to help students internalize the feedback. New images might come up that help students with academics.
- An essential question can be anchored in the classroom to prompt students to think about the visualizations:

    How does making pictures in your mind during feedback help you to understand the feedback?

Feedback Activities for Predicting

Prediction is a great feedback strategy. It is more than having students figure out what they need to do next. It is also about having students make predictions about what the next goals need to be. It helps students make new inquiries about what they could do to make their work better and why. Predicting also facilitates *what-if…* questions; e.g., *What if I did X instead of Y?*

- As students go through this process of thinking about their work more deeply, they are provided with opportunities to understand the content more comprehensively. Since questions can be an important part of the Feedback for Predicting process, Feedback Dice or Feedback Cards can be used to help think about the kinds of questions that need to be asked.
- Mind-mapping is also an excellent strategy students can use to map out and brainstorm possibilities for predicting the next step, because it requires them to use evidence from their work to determine why their work might need to take a new or different direction.
- Exit tickets are an excellent way for students to make predictions about what they need to do next, based on feedback about their academics.

Feedback Activities for Inferring

Inferring is a skill that is based on prior knowledge and experience. Feedback can help hone this skill by prompting students to engage in text, cueing prior knowledge and experience. Students need to make inferences from feedback to make meaning as well.

Using inferences as feedback is about students applying their content knowledge and feedback received to understanding what they need to do next. Feedback provides the scaffolds necessary to help students learn and grow. Quite often, we infer these scaffolds based on what we are taught to see about the work we are doing. A feedback-friendly classroom builds these schemas so that students can make more meaningful inferences about the content and tasks being completed.

The feedback becomes visible and explicit, helping students build new schema for inferencing.

- The feedback gleaned from the activities like Feedback Dice or Feedback Cards can help students read between the lines and make clearer inferences. Taking the information and combining it with personal knowledge is an important way of creating meaning surrounding academic content, socialization, and personal development.
- An essential question can be anchored in the classroom to help students metacognitively think about the inferring process:

  How does feedback help us to understand what we are learning?

- Students assess what they are experiencing from their work, think about what they already know, and then make their inferences about their learning. Students can use the Inferring from Feedback template on page 75.
- Using the Think–Pair–Feedback strategy, students can work together to develop a working definition of inferring. Be sure to allow for individual think time. Then, if appropriate, it might be valuable to have students work with a partner to verbalize their thinking, share with the whole group, and give more feedback.

Feedback Activities for Questioning

Questions can be a very powerful form of feedback. They can cause you or another person to think about things not previously considered about academic content or work being handed in. Questions can be considered for use in any strategy, including talking circles, Think–Pair–Feedback, exit tickets, reflection forms, use of artifacts, and more. They can be generated in a number of ways: you can use Feedback Dice, create your own, or draw from the lists below.

Questions for the teacher include

- *How do we engage students with feedback for learning?*
- *How do we help students use their background knowledge to deepen their connections to feedback?*
- *How can we help students use feedback to make deeper connections?*

Questions for students can be discussed in a talking circle, might include

- *How does using your background knowledge help you understand?*
- *How does making connections between what you know and what you read help you understand?*

Questions on Feedback Cards can be used to help keep students focused on providing feedback on the personal reflection of the academic work being conducted.

What have you learned?	How do you know you have learned?
What do you do or think about differently now?	What are you still confused about?
How have you created new knowledge from your past experiences and new content?	What goal do you still need to reach?

How have you already taken steps toward the goal?	Do you need to build new goals?

Feedback Activities for Reflecting

Reflection can occur at any time in the learning process. It is often used after a student receives an assignment or test that has been graded. After a student receives this feedback, they use a reflection form to record their reflections. The forms can be handed back to the teacher to make sure that there is congruency between what the teacher thinks about the feedback and what the student thinks about the feedback.

- It is valuable for students to reflect on feedback they have received during any of the feedback activities, including those using Feedback Dice or Cards.
- Use a feedback think-aloud. In a think-aloud, the teacher models the thinking that leads to reaching learning goals and successful outcomes. The think-aloud is a feedback strategy in and of itself. You can apply this strategy to model to your students various feedback processes. For example, as you conduct think-alouds as they relate to comprehension strategies, you can also integrate feedback as it pertains to the task, process, and self. Use the Observation Template on page 76 to record the connection between comprehension strategies and feedback.
- Use sentence starters to help students reflect on their feedback:

  I saw…
  What I know about the work/task is …
  What I think is…
  This connects to previous knowledge by…
  I now wonder…

- Exit tickets that prompt reflection on feedback would include questions like the following:

  What message did you try to convey with your feedback today?
  How did you feel about your work/your peer's work?
  What behaviors did you use to express how you felt?
  What vocabulary did you use?
  How did your feedback connect to your background knowledge and experiences?
  How did you help a friend?

Additional Academic Strategies for Feedback

Academics other than literacy and comprehension can also benefit from more focused feedback based on the unique language and processes relevant to a particular subject area. For instance, in math there could be a focus on important processes. In science, the focus is likely to be more on the scientific method, and in social studies the focus might be on unique areas of disciplinary thinking.

Math Processes and Feedback

We all are aware of instructional strategies for math, including collaborating, scaffolding, sharing new resources, guiding, and modelling. But we might not consider these strategies as embedding meaningful feedback that fosters a feedback-friendly classroom. Feedback activities can be used to help support academic understanding in math.

Talking circles are a good place to start when it comes to learning about the math processes. Brainstorming what students already know is a great way to co-create the language that students will use. The language that is important and culturally relevant while involved in the problem-solving processes could be quite different from that listed in the curriculum document. While we want to ensure that our students are indeed using shared, appropriate language, it is equally important that the language is relevant and understandable by children, is culturally responsive, and is shared in ways that are meaningful to the knowledge and experiences of the students in the class.

The following feedback strategies can be used and visually shared in the classroom to help students choose the math processes and problem-solving strategies most appropriate to them:

- Think–Pair–Feedback, page 44
- Mind-Mapping, page 43
- Stop/Start/Continue, page 45
- Plus/Idea/Next Step, page 46
- Two Stars and a Wish, page 46
- One to Glow, One to Grow, page 46

In this form of pedagogical documentation, you could also make brief anecdotal notes about the learning and feedback being shared.

The math processes that students become aware of include reasoning and proving, reflecting, selecting tools and computational strategies, connecting, representing, problem-solving, and communication. You can use a chart like Math Processes and Feedback for Academics on page 77 to record the feedback strategies you use to promote academic learning in math.

Scientific Processes and Feedback

Feedback for scientific processes is also significant. Science literacy is a key component of learning in 21st-century learning. Asking questions, making hypotheses, conducting experiments, recording results, making conclusions, and reflecting are necessary steps of the scientific process. You can use a chart like Scientific Processes and Feedback for Academics on page 78 to record the feedback strategies you use to promote academic learning in math.

Students can use the Scientific Method template on page 79 to record and reflect on their feedback, and to consider where they need to go next.

Social Studies and Feedback

In many curricula, social studies is organized in terms of significance, cause and consequence, continuity and change, patterns and trends, interrelationships, and perspective. Again, you can use the Social Studies Processes and Feedback for Academics chart on page 80 to keep track of where and when you use strategies and activities to elicit feedback for and between your students. Depending on the strategy you use, the language used can focus feedback along these lines of disciplinary thinking.

Feedback Strategies for 21st-Century Skills Checklist

Subject _____

Big Idea: _____

Feedback Strategy/Activity	Collaboration	Inquiry	Problem-solving	Global Connections	Cultural Responsiveness

Pembroke Publishers © 2015 *The Feedback-Friendly Classroom* by Deborah McCallum ISBN 978-1-55138-304-0

Inferring from Feedback

What I read/see	What I already know	Feedback I received	What I can infer

Observation Template

Think-Aloud Strategy	Feedback elicited on Task	Feedback elicited on Process	Feedback elicited on Self
Questioning			
Inferring			
Visualizing			
Predicting			
Main Idea			
Connecting			
Reflecting			
Summarizing			

Math Processes and Feedback for Academics

Math Processes	Feedback Strategies for Collaboration	Feedback Strategies for Inquiry	Feedback Strategies for Problem-solving	Feedback Strategies for Global Connections	Feedback Strategies for Cultural Responsiveness
Reasoning and Proving					
Reflecting					
Selecting Tools and Computational Strategies					
Connecting					
Representing					
Problem-solving					
Communication					

Pembroke Publishers © 2015 *The Feedback-Friendly Classroom* by Deborah McCallum ISBN 978-1-55138-304-0

Scientific Processes and Feedback for Academics

Steps of the Scientific Process	Feedback Strategies for Collaboration	Feedback Strategies for Inquiry	Feedback Strategies for Problem-solving	Feedback Strategies for Global Connections	Feedback Strategies for Cultural Responsiveness
Question					
Hypothesis					
Experiment					
Results					
Conclusions					

Scientific Method

Scientific Method	My Work	My Feedback Reflection
Ask a Question		
Make a Hypothesis		
Conduct Experiment		
Record Results		
Make Conclusions		
Was your hypothesis right?		

Pembroke Publishers © 2015 *The Feedback-Friendly Classroom* by Deborah McCallum ISBN 978-1-55138-304-0

Social Studies Processes and Feedback for Academics

Disciplinary Thinking for Social Studies	Feedback Strategies for Collaboration	Feedback Strategies for Inquiry	Feedback Strategies for Problem-solving	Feedback Strategies for Global Connections	Feedback Strategies for Cultural Responsiveness
Significance					
Cause and Consequence					
Continuity and Change					
Patterns and Trends					
Interrelationships					
Perspective					

Pembroke Publishers © 2015 *The Feedback-Friendly Classroom* by Deborah McCallum ISBN 978-1-55138-304-0

6

Feedback for Socialization

We see in our Kindergarten classrooms a renewed emphasis on the importance of play. Play is an important activity whereby students learn valuable feedback from their peers in terms of appropriate behaviors, cooperation, competition, and different points of view.

Academic learning is not the only learning that takes place within the classroom. Students learn just as much, if not more, from interacting with their peers. The feedback that students get from others has a profound impact on behavior, including learning behavior. Students learn about cooperation, competition, and more, based on feedback from others in the classroom. This feedback is occurring every day, and I believe that we can work to integrate language and activities that help make this as productive and positive as possible. Socialization is just as important as academics, and it can have a very profound impact on academics if it is not addressed within the classroom.

The strategies we decide to use will help our students to trust their own instincts based on their own knowledge and experiences. It is important that we use feedback strategies for socialization to help students frame their feedback in socially acceptable ways in our feedback-friendly classroom. Language is essential to this process. Therefore, talking circles are an excellent way to develop the kind of language and vocabulary that will be appropriate to the culture of your feedback-friendly classroom. (See Chapter 8 for more on feedback language.)

How we speak to others can have profound effects on mindsets and behaviors. When our traditional school system was built, a lot of the feedback that we had to give was to produce fixed mindsets and compliance to serve the economy and values of the Industrial Era. Students were to learn from the teacher, who conveyed the information and knowledge students needed to be successful. Students were not permitted to engage with each other for the purposes of collaborative learning and knowledge-building processes. Our learning had to be fixed because fixed mindsets were essential for the means of production. Students would master the set knowledge and skills they needed for the jobs they would hold for their entire lives.

In the 21st century, we need students who are flexible with their learning, and who can acquire new knowledge all the time for a career that will consist of many different types of work. Students need to learn appropriate strategies to effectively share feedback with each other, critically think about the feedback, and understand the processes for dealing with the feedback to build knowledge, improve, and grow. In a knowledge economy, technologies abound, and information is freely shared. Some of this information is in the form of feedback. Therefore, it becomes an important 21st-century skill to be able to collaborate with others in the manner of giving, receiving, and seeking appropriate feedback to build the new knowledges that our world needs. Our students need to be able to interact in meaningful ways with their peers. This fosters skills that they will take with them into other situations—situations that will serve them appropriately in the future. We need our students to be problem-solvers, to be resourceful, and to be able to connect well with others. They need to be able to communicate and work well with others to build new knowledge. Feedback is the cornerstone of honing these processes.

Each student has important things to contribute to the classroom. This is not something that all students naturally understand. Some students are quieter and participate in different ways. It is through communicative strategies that students can learn about the knowledge and special pieces of themselves that they can contribute to the classroom. Effective ways of giving, receiving, and seeking feedback also give information about the wonderful things that all students can contribute to the classroom.

The Feedback for Socialization chart on page 85 can be used to keep track of the various feedback strategies you use for socialization with your students. You can use it to list each strategy you use to monitor the 21st-century skills that you are also covering.

Nothing makes me happier than seeing students who have been working together all year come to understand how to use each other as valuable resources.

Play and Collaboration

Exploration, makerspaces, discovery, nutrition breaks, and more can be seen as potential forms of play within the classroom. Feedback is something that students naturally obtain from their peers during play. In the context of play, you can provide activities that help students understand, be metacognitive, and give positive feedback to one another about their social and communication skills.

Promoting collaboration requires effective feedback strategies. These strategies go beyond traditional methods of providing basic rewards and punishments for various behaviors. It involves complex social dynamics and, therefore, requires feedback strategies that address these complexities. Feedback Dice or Feedback Cards can be used to identify some of the complexities, and make the complexities explicit through open dialogue.

Feedback Cards

With Feedback Cards, you can use language and visual prompts to help students to give specific feedback that promotes safe and friendly classrooms through socialization:

Thank you for…	*What I appreciated most was…*
What I heard you say is…	What are you thinking?
What do you already know about the topic?	What would you add?
What would you change?	What do you think a next step would be?

Feedback Dice

Feedback Dice can help students understand more difficult and complex emotions and behaviors, including anger, jealousy, hurt feelings, anxiety, misunderstanding, withdrawal, fitting in, and power struggles. Understanding these different feelings, emotions, and behaviors can help students make better sense of not just their own feelings, but also the feelings of others.

They can also help to freeze certain social cues in time to make them more explicit for students. This provides an opportunity for students to look at them, think about them, and gain valuable feedback from teachers and peers in a safe classroom environment before going back out into a play situation.

Feedback Dice using these prompts can be used collaboratively to get discussions going. When students are finished, they can find a way to make the feedback visible and share ideas and key learnings with the class. The first die can have basic scenarios on each side:

- a situation in which someone is hurt
- experiencing envy or jealousy
- a power struggle
- a situation involving sharing
- a situation involving exclusion
- trying to fit in

It is up to the group to take one of those basic ideas and create a role-play situation to look at more deeply and think about metacognitively. Dice 2, 4, and 5 can be used, as usual, to prompt and guide feedback:

- Dice 2: Appreciation
- Dice 4: Question Word
- Dice 5: Next Word

Conversations

Questions can be shared through classroom discussion and conversation, or used in a graphic organizer or form that allows students to explore their experiences with feedback in social situations. Making our thinking visible and sharing our thinking in safe ways is imperative, because this provides valuable feedback to others in the class:

What do you think about how the media portrays your gender/your age/dreams you should have for yourself?
What messages do parents send?
What messages does school transmit to students? How does it do this?
What messages do you get from your friends?

These ideas can be shared through conversations, rich classroom discussions, on posters, through digital presentations. You can also set up shared online documents or poster paper around the room for students to anonymously share their ideas.

After the thinking has been made visible and shared in a safe manner, new questions can be asked:

> Which of the class ideas shared are realistically attainable?
> Which are *should*s and which are *hopeful*s?

It is vital to understand that using feedback to improve socialization is a process that occurs over time. Students must always come back to the process and evolve with it. The feedback process helps students internalize and use feedback from others about socialization. It is also learning about what is right for them as individuals, and as cultural beings in their own right.

Feedback for Socialization

Feedback Activity/Strategy	Collaboration	Inquiry	Problem-solving	Global Connections	Cultural Responsiveness

Pembroke Publishers © 2015 *The Feedback-Friendly Classroom* by Deborah McCallum ISBN 978-1-55138-304-0

7

Feedback for Development

Strategies for Development

I cannot remember the first time that I heard this: *What we teach students is not what they learn.* I think it is a very powerful statement. Every student comes to the class with different knowledge sets. Some of what we teach are what they already know. Further, what one person learns can be completely different from what another person learns. We end up a rich and diverse classroom we can tap into for new perspectives and ideas that can propel feedback and learning forward in new ways. We do not need to control everything. We can create our lesson and unit plans but, at the end of the day, we cannot submit these plans as proof of what each student learned. We need to have strategies that actively help students and teachers alike monitor the learning that *is* taking place. More importantly, we need to cultivate students' skills to be able to monitor their learning that is taking place.

We can help students internalize critical learning behaviors by letting them know what they did well, by always helping ourselves and our students focus on what was done well. When students are aware of what they are doing well and how they are doing it well, they are more likely to be able to apply these skills when they do experience difficulty in learning. Also, if we teach students to look for other possibilities in learning behaviors and teach them new patterns of learning, then we can help them become more independent and not solely reliant on the teacher (Johnston, 2004).

The truth is that we know all too well about the many different behaviors that come to the classroom. It is always a learning process to understand someone else's feelings and personal goals, let alone our own motivations. More difficult can be being able to monitor the effects of our responses on someone else. Even deeper are the processes that we use to self-regulate and help someone else to regulate. When we think about mental health issues and other behavioral disorders, we need to make sure that we are differentiating our feedback strategies to meet our students' needs. Not every student will be working toward the same social goals. Therefore different feedback strategies will be useful at different times and for different purposes. We also know that various populations are more vulnerable than others, depending upon various factors, including socio-economic status, impacts of residential schools, urban vs. rural, and access to supports.

Our strategies for socialization need to focus on the positive aspects of someone's behavior, then suggestions for a next step. These can include One to Glow, One to Grow (see page 46) and Plus/Idea/Next Step (see page 46). In general, we are interested in behaviors that show the student as a learner and a friend, and as someone with personal agency in the classroom. Therefore, we need to focus on the strategies that can help promote this.

Scaffolding

Feedback should never be used to embarrass a student in front of his/her peers for behaviors considered bad.

Scaffolding is an excellent strategy that can help you raise the bar for a student in terms of development. The important thing about scaffolding is that it helps students to meet their goals gradually. It is through feedback that we determine the scaffolds.

- A visual depiction of the progression might be beneficial to help a student "see" how far they have moved up the steps, if you can find a visual that works for you and your student.
- If the student is self-aware, the steps can be co-created.
- If you use this activity as a class activity, it can be an excellent way to help students see the relationships between the steps to improving behavior. For instance, if there is a problem at recess then, as a group or class, students can work on the baby steps required to do their best and visualize next steps in development of a solution. If a student is having personal issues, for example with frustration or inability to understand teacher instructions, this could be done privately.
- Steps can be used to understand basic language and strategies that will help take development to the next level.

The thing to keep in mind is that this can be a very sensitive area, particularly if the student is experiencing a great deal of stress at home or school that is affecting development. Therefore, in addition to promoting a safe and positive environment in the feedback-friendly classroom, it is crucial to keep open communication with parents and home and with other key people who might be needed to help the student.

Monitoring Learning

Using a graphic organizer to record observations about different types of learning behaviors is an excellent strategy for student use. It can be used for behaviors already executed by the student, or be based in observation of other learning behaviors in class. Students can record detailed observations about what happened or what could happen. This can supply you with useful information about the skills to focus on next in the learning process.

Help students use the perspective of a theory of action; see page 26 for more. Have students use the Theory of Action for Students organizer on page 94 to consider cause and consequence, and their bearing on what happens next.

Feedback for Self-Regulation

When learners are self-regulating, they are monitoring their knowledge development and their development of their understanding. Therefore, students need effective strategies that elicit the kind of feedback that helps them to self-regulate. Activities that help students set goals and plan their learning are essential. How students plan their learning will also affect the way that they look for information and how they will understand the information.

Scaffolding, conferencing, Think–Pair–Feedback, visual displays, and visual cues support self-regulated learning. For instance, using a visual to show how many steps might be in a process can help students make more meaningful connections between the steps. Research has shown this to work much more effectively than if feedback is just described. Placing Feedback Cards on the whiteboard, chart paper, and word walls can serve as visual reminders.

Sometimes, our learning goals are specifically linked with self-regulation. With our help, students learn to manage their attention and apply it to the knowledge and skills they are learning. We hope that their self-awareness is heightened to help them better take responsibility for their learning. Feedback for learning goals and social learning is important, but we also need to focus the feedback on student self-regulation and metacognition. Self-regulation not only promotes knowledge and understanding of skills, but is also a critical element of motivation and helping students to become responsible for their learning journey. According to Zimmerman (2002), self-regulation can be organized into three main categories:

- forethought
- performance
- self-reflection

Therefore, feedback strategies can help students focus on

- the processes they need to use before the learning begins; e.g., analyzing the task that needs to be done and their motivation for learning
- their performance
- their ability to evaluate themselves and their work against the learning goals

The Feedback for Development chart on page 95 can help you keep track of when and how you use the feedback strategies for socialization.

To help with the overall process of self-regulation, students will need to have regular, ongoing access to feedback from teachers and peers. They also need to practice giving and receiving feedback regularly. The strategies, therefore, need to focus on the process of learning, and not the outcome.

Some students have difficulty with self-regulation simply because they are unable to experience progress. Appropriate feedback is important throughout the learning process to demonstrate how students are experiencing success along the journey toward learning goals. We don't need to wait until the learning goals are met. The feedback-friendly classroom helps students learn to self-assess throughout the learning process, as feedback strategies are used to demonstrate that learning and growth are happening. We can help students self-regulate by providing engaging strategies, topics, and ideas for helping them self-assess. Opportunities for self-assessment can begin right when students start planning for learning.

Effective feedback strategies for improving self-regulation are those that can help students understand learning goals and set new personal learning goals. Also, they help students plan their next steps, focus on vital concepts and elements that will lead to success, become more organized with their thinking, learn about consequences, develop growth mindsets, and transfer learning skills to new contexts.

In our classrooms, it is only through social-emotional practice that we can embed character education, growth mindsets, and basic social skills for collaboration when we allow students to interact together in our classrooms. Deliberate and explicit strategies to help students practice this communication in effective ways through a feedback-friendly classroom is essential.

Goal-Setting

Self-regulated learning is a process by which students monitor, regulate, and control their learning behaviors and knowledge to achieve goals. Feedback is absolutely essential to help students set and work toward learning goals. According to Regan (2013), successful goal-setting has four components:

1. Setting a goal for learning
2. Self-monitoring performance
3. Developing and following self-instructions
4. Reinforcing performance

See Chapter 8 for more on goal-setting in the classroom.

There are negative consequences if we teach only to expectations without goal-setting. Teaching to curricular expectations will inevitably mean positive feedback for some students but negative feedback for others. Goals help us focus on what is most important and help students focus on and understand what they are doing well. They also help students and teachers understand when a student has reached beyond themselves.

Students can use the Feedback Dice or Feedback Cards to help formulate questions for goal-setting. These types of questions can be explicitly posed in a talking circle, on a reflection card, or on a learning contract. Answers can also be placed on cue cards or sticky notes and stuck to large pieces of chart paper hung up around the room, each with one of the different questions at the top. This helps make the learning visible but also does not single out any students.

What are my goals?	What is working?	What is not working?
What have I learned?	What do I still need to learn?	How will I learn that?

Each goal has three parts:

1. behavior: what is to be learned or performed
2. evaluation: how much and how often behavior will be demonstrated
3. circumstances: when we demonstrate behavior; how we know when the behavior is learned

Therefore, it is important to choose activities that will give meaningful feedback for goal-setting. Talking circles, visualization, Plus/Idea/Next Step, Think–Share–Feedback, Two Stars and a Wish, and templates for success criteria used in conjunction with reflection cards are valuable.

As students interact with the feedback strategies, they can record their reflections and keep them in a journal or portfolio and come back to them over time. This is a useful idea to help students internalize the crucial components of socialization processes, reinforce with feedback, and then begin the process of self-regulation toward those goals.

Conflict

It is important for students to understand that disagreement is normal. We handle conflict by helping students break down their discussions into smaller parts. We have the power to turn student attention toward the significance of group processes and strategies that promote feedback and other skills for dealing with conflict. We teach students that their differing perspectives are valuable resources for their learning.

Conflict can be deliberately set up for students to work through, so they learn the patterns of feedback that promote learning and respect. A process can be planned by which a problem needs to be solved, and students can collaborate by rehearsing the feedback processes. This helps to build relationships and make them aware that we accomplish our learning collaboratively. The higher quality the collaboration, the better the learning outcomes. Role-plays are excellent strategies for these purposes. As teachers and students co-construct activities and situations that students can use to practice dealing with conflicting viewpoints, we also offer prompts to help students practice and to cue new lines of thinking.

On page 96 is a Resolving Conflict template that outlines a process that resembles an inquiry. It involves identifying up to three possible perspectives and brainstorming solutions. Blank Feedback Cards can be laminated with magnets and placed up on the whiteboard or stuck to chart paper to make this exercise more visible.

Feedback promotes cognitive change when learners must confront and coordinate conflicting viewpoints. The fact is that disagreement moves student thinking forward more than agreement. Students learn not merely about tolerance, but that differences can be personally beneficial to us. We can normalize what it means. Feedback helps us see alternative perspectives and helps us refocus our inquiries and flesh out and articulate our position more fully.

It is inevitable that the culture of the classroom will have conflicting feedback messages. This is where we help students effectively give, receive, and seek feedback, always linking it directly to their personal goals. We can motivate our students to understand that there are multiple ways of knowing in the world and that even the teacher does not necessarily have the one right way of knowing.

When students are giving each other feedback, we don't need to make them responsible for correcting other students. Feedback needs to go beyond this level of task feedback, so that students are not responsible for correcting their peers. Instead, we want students to learn to communicate to help make connections, consider alternative points of view, reflect, and integrate new information.

There are essentially three processes of feedback: receiving a message, processing the message, sending the message. When a student gives feedback to a peer, that student will not know how the other learner will perceive the feedback. We can encourage vital listening behaviors to increase the likelihood that information can be processed in ways that are meaningful to the student. We can provide role-play activities for dealing with potential issues before they develop, to guide a repertoire of behaviors to move learning forward.

Motivation

Helping students become motivated or stay motivated is a natural part of the feedback-friendly classroom. Learners feel more motivated when they have opportunities to experience autonomy, have feelings of competence, and relate to one another (Ryan & Deci, 2000). Therefore, feedback strategies can promote active and volitional learning (instead of passive and controlled learning), provide different kinds of feedback, and propel learning forward (Ryan & Deci, p. 55).

Motivation is inextricably linked with frustration. If students experience too much frustration, their motivation for learning will suffer and so will achievement levels. One of the goals of the feedback-friendly classroom is to use the

How do we know if feedback will lower a person's self-esteem? As humans, we all have a need to feel accepted, rather than rejected. We need to help our students feel valued and accepted through our feedback.

90

strategies to keep frustration levels to a minimum. Feedback cards can be used to help students self-regulate by simplifying the tasks, helping students focus on separate parts of a problem, and providing support for the things done well. This goes a long way toward reducing frustration for students, and also allows students to make mistakes without mistakes being evaluated. It is motivating for students when they know that they can be vulnerable and accepted when learning.

We can also make a distinction between intrinsic and extrinsic motivation. If we want students who love the learning process, then we can reinforce it by embedding feedback into our daily interactions that emphasize the process over the product, the learning processes more than the final mark. By helping each other grow and learn, and become better, students develop intrinsic motivation for the learning process.

Handling Negative Feedback

Teachers sometimes need to provide feedback next-steps that highlight what to do better; students sometimes perceive this as negative feedback. When students give feedback in a feedback-friendly classroom, we want them to focus on only the positive aspects of someone's work. When working in group activities and sharing ideas, we want students to acknowledge positively others' ideas, but not assess their work; this is the job of the teacher. In a feedback-friendly classroom we want to encourage students to build on others' ideas with new ideas, share what is working well, change what they do based on what they can see from others, and ask questions. This is another reason why making work visible is critical. Opportunities to practice positive feedback can occur throughout each stage of our lesson planning.

It is very difficult for anyone to hear negative feedback. Sometimes it depends on how feedback is presented. Therefore we need strategies to help students deliver feedback in positive ways. Practicing different kinds of feedback through role-play and Feedback Cards is essential. Feedback Cards help students practice the talk, questions, body language, and ideas that are important in the feedback process. Practice making feedback concise and specific, and analyzing the task, not the person or their personality, clothes, etc. The Productive and Unproductive Feedback template on page 97 can be filled out as a group or individually to begin the thinking. It can be used to co-create the success criteria. We always want students to compare to the success criteria and learning goals.

In a feedback-friendly classroom we don't want students to give feedback based on different criteria or no criteria. We need explicit criteria. We need to be explicit in our language, visuals, and demonstrations when creating our success criteria and learning goals. If we are not conscious of this and lack explicit criteria for behaviors and feedback, students will fill in the blanks themselves. This can have devastating effects if we are not careful. If most of the feedback a student receives from peers with regard to learning is incorrect, then we have a lot of work to do to make learning goals explicit. This ensures that the entire classroom culture can work to establish a respectful, specific, and constructive climate that fosters natural discussions and behaviors that propel learning forward.

A feedback-friendly classroom is not about comparing students to each other. We need to celebrate each other's differences and work to highlight those differences. However, how do we handle it when students do perceive negative feedback, either intentional or unintentional? One-on-one conversations with

Do not use charts in the classroom that compare students to one another, as this can be damaging to self-esteem.

the teacher are critical for students to be able to continue the feedback process, mediated by the teacher. Preemptive talking circles can also take place early on in the school year and throughout the term to help students make new connections and engage in metacognition about their words and behaviors.

Feedback Cards for Development

These sample feedback cards can be valuable for helping students to continue to give feedback in developmentally appropriate ways.

Feedback Cards for Growth Mindsets

The following feedback cards provide visuals and prompts to help centre student thinking around promoting growth mindsets and positive thinking. It is vital in helping students self-reflect and create minds-on, visual cues to remember the power of their social behaviors. This helps with feelings of safety and reduces judgment used in the feedback process as well.

Yet…	Next time I will…	It is okay to make mistakes.
I am learning more when I make mistakes and fail.	I have courage to take risks with my learning.	My learning and attitude are more important than my grades.

Feedback Cards for Character Development

Feedback Cards like these can help with thinking about how character development relates to behavior, thoughts, and feelings; and academics, socialization, and development.

I showed honesty when…	I showed trust when…	I showed cooperation when…
I showed integrity when…	I showed effective communication when…	I made a positive connection to another person when…
I was a good citizen when…	I collaborated when…	I shared with another person by…

Feedback Cards for Feelings

Each card will have a visual in the middle, a keyword at the bottom, and a description on the back.

Happy	Sad	Frustrated	Scared
Shy	Curious	Bored	Silly

Safe	Unsafe	Calm	Anxious
Nervous	Blah	Jealous	Embarrassed
Sorry	Worried	Proud	Excited
Thankful	Terrific	Confused	Uncertain
Hopeless	Surprised	Self-Conscious	Satisfied

Theory of Action for Students

	Basic Situation	Additional Details
If this happens		
Then this happens		
My next steps should be…		

Pembroke Publishers © 2015 *The Feedback-Friendly Classroom* by Deborah McCallum ISBN 978-1-55138-304-0

Feedback for Development

Feedback Activity/Strategy	Collaboration	Inquiry	Problem-solving	Global Connections	Cultural Responsiveness
for Goal-Setting					
for Resolving Conflict					

Resolving Conflict

Conflict			
Inquiry about Conflict	1	2	3
Perspectives on the Conflict	1	2	3
Possible Solutions	1	2	3

Pembroke Publishers © 2015 *The Feedback-Friendly Classroom* by Deborah McCallum ISBN 978-1-55138-304-0

Productive and Unproductive Feedback

	Productive	Unproductive
Sentence Starters		
Verbs		
Task		
Question		
Tone of Voice		
Body Language		

8

Creating the Feedback-Friendly Classroom

Consider these questions for reflection:

- How do you begin to build an effective feedback-friendly classroom that will support the needs of all learners?
- What feelings does this evoke?
- What assessments have you planned for your class: formative and summative?
- Have you identified the learning goals?
- How will you share feedback?
- What interventions would you put in place to foster a feedback-friendly classroom?

What thoughts are running through your head? How did you see or hear yourself responding? What skills do you have to manage the situation? What skills are you lacking? What do you observe about the class? How are your observations affecting your ability to give and receive feedback? How do you know whether your teaching and the student learning will be helpful?

Answering these questions is difficult, particularly before you have had a chance to truly get to know your students. Sometimes, we cannot even attempt to comprehend what a feedback-friendly classroom will look like until we begin the year-long journey together as a classroom community. It is important to realize that loops of feedback are already occurring within the classroom and that they can either help or hinder the learning process. Teachers can be proactive and set the stage for friendlier feedback that leads to greater outcomes for students.

Now that we have decided to make our classrooms feedback-friendly, we have to address certain perceptions and barriers that can significantly affect our ability to integrate meaningful feedback into the classroom. Research has found that teachers perceive time management, classroom organization, and classroom management as barriers to giving feedback (van den Bergh, 2013). If we take a moment to unpack these barriers, we get an idea of where we need to focus.

Classroom organization can be a barrier because it takes a lot of time to keep students organized in class. A feedback-friendly classroom needs clear guidelines for where everything goes and set routines for how to organize materials. The more organized students can be, the better the feedback you will be able to model and the more time students can be engaged in feedback-friendly strategies. At the same time, a feedback-friendly classroom is flexible, in that it bends with the needs of the students. The strategies and students can be organized differently from day to day, depending on the social contexts and relationships at play.

Classroom management skills are essential to a feedback-friendly classroom. Students need consistent routines so they can predict what is expected of them. It has been found that almost 60% of teachers believe that feedback needs to activate and stimulate work and thinking (van den Bergh, 2013). The implications are more-directive feedback; however, this contrasts with most self-regulative feedback common to a feedback-friendly classroom. Strategies that become embedded into the learning process to incorporate self-regulative feedback will benefit all in the classroom. All learners benefit because they learn to monitor group behaviors, make the classroom safer, and make it easier to build in social-learning and feedback processes.

Instructional Design

My instructional design has evolved by looking at my teaching through the lens of feedback that infuses the classroom. It has prompted me to think about the most meaningful ways for students to construct knowledge for learning, both as individuals and as key components of the larger social environment in the classroom. My curriculum planning can no longer be about organizing lessons according to subject matter. The feedback has become integral to my planning of instruction, as well as integrative, i.e., as a tool for integrating ideas. Feedback is the glue that holds together learning goals and subject matter, and cements them into the lives and previous knowledge of the students.

Expectations, success criteria, and assessment are not ends in and of themselves. Feedback for learning and a growth mindset are the goals of the entire feedback process. Students can interact in meaningful ways to build their understandings around the subject matter, and help each other to drive learning forward. I now try to approach the curriculum expectations from a feedback angle, from which the feedback is built into the social frameworks of the class.

When developing and designing my curriculum, I always start with questions: *How will students see themselves reflected in their learning? And how will I help craft inquiries to promote student innovation and reflection?* I believe that how we plan our curriculum and the questions we ask will determine ultimately how we achieve our goals. Regardless of how innovative we want to get, we still need to have a basic sequence of steps, including purpose, design, implementation, and assessment (Ornstein, 2013, p. 8). From these steps flow the important questions we need to ask to elicit the desired discussions, answers, and output from our learners. We are faced with inquiries that extend from *what* we teach to *how* we should teach. We need questions that motivate students to move beyond regurgitating knowledge toward applying the knowledge in creative ways and engaging in creative problem-solving. Depending on our personal definitions of curriculum, the questions we ask can position us as experts or as facilitators for our students. It will also determine how students will be introduced and initiated into the curriculum.

There are multiple ways to interpret the curriculum, and all have the ability to bring much value to the classroom. However, not all educational goals can be known. Therefore, think of the goals and curriculum as evolving entities, changing and manifesting in real time, rather than being thoroughly planned well in advance.

We all have goals for our students to achieve the best grades and scores they can on tests and other assessments. But this is merely a snapshot and often does not say much about the actual processes of learning. How can formal and informal feedback strategies support learning processes that work toward goals vs. final grades? I think if we can direct our learning toward goals with feedback-friendly strategies, then we can ensure that our students are learning and growing and helping each other to learn and grow in meaningful ways. This is a big undertaking because it means that you are actively building the feedback culture of your classroom right from the beginning. It may feel a bit contrived at first, but it is essential to take the steps that will eventually become a natural part of the classroom. Feedback should be a natural extension of our teaching and instructional practices, as we build routines, accountable talk, and communities of students who can learn to support each other's thinking and learning.

As we grow away from the mere act of just covering the expectations and obtaining a grade, we use feedback to slow down the process and uncover the individual complexities that arise within our unique learning contexts. When we move beyond traditional views of equating feedback with charts with stars, checkmarks, and written feedback on a test, we can use it as a way to validate our jobs as teachers.

Grades can have the potential to put an abrupt end to the feedback process. When we want to promote working to help each other to learn, grow, and build a community of learners, a feedback-friendly classroom, we teach that grades are not the end, just a part of the process. We then need to continue to act on that feedback and interact with it to continue the journey. Giving students grades—especially too early in the learning process—erodes trust, diminishes relationships, and fosters unhealthy power dynamics within the classroom. If we give students a grade before the process has had a chance to cycle through, then the feedback will often be meaningless. Why would a student continue with the feedback process if they already know their grade, and there is no additional interaction with the feedback? A grade is final. We are required to hand them out, but in a feedback-friendly classroom, it is something best left until the very end of the term. And when we do hand out final grades, we want them to justify the feedback that has been shared and disseminated within in the classroom. We need to make sure that the final grade supports the learning that stemmed from the feedback processes; therefore, we need to ensure that our strategies are of high quality. Feedback processes are happening whether we acknowledge them or not. If we recognize that they are occurring and strive to implement the strategies that foster relationships, positive and growth mindsets, and appropriate language for learning, then there is a much higher chance that quality learning will take place.

Hidden Curriculum

If we go by the assumption that the curriculum incorporates more than the mandated curriculum syllabi, but also the experiences and interactions that take place within the classroom, then we must also consider the fact that the curriculum can end up being both what we plan and what we do not plan. We do not plan on the myriad interactions that will take place within a classroom. We might inadvertently dismiss the power of the classroom informal social interactions. And this null, or hidden, curriculum exists, even if we are not planning for it, practicing

Since a teacher cannot work with every student at all times of the day, we need students to be able to learn and embed feedback skills. The abler they are to do this, the better they will self-regulate their learning and think critically about new learning when they have left the classroom and are out in the world.

it, or using it. How students interact with the curriculum can be harnessed via key strategies and language to gain knowledge of what students implicitly know and how they can hone those skills to improve the learning process. For instance, students can learn to be aware of body language or tone of voice to help them become more self-aware. Also, students can share explicit vocabulary and sentence starters until a new shared language is cultivated. Regardless of whether we acknowledge this or not, it still can send out powerful information to others.

The hidden expectations of our curriculum are the ones that determine the unintended outcomes of schooling. They also elicit unintended feedback. The unintended feedback will influence learning just as much as the intended feedback. Just because students are unaware of the feedback they are giving and receiving does not mean that they are not giving and receiving it. It does not mean that it does not affect learning within the classroom.

There are real implications for society when we assume absolute authority in our curriculum and teaching, and do not question the norms, skills, and knowledge therein. When we look at the curriculum that is restricted to the objectives of the school as the blueprint for achievement, and we do not question those blueprints, we are at risk of omitting valuable cultures and experiences, norms, knowledge, and skills. The dominant ideology does not need to be directed from the teacher. The feedback evenly spreads through the breadth of experiences and ideals within the classroom. Students can harness it to understand what they do know and what they have experienced. They are all equally able to contribute to the classroom learning environment.

Inquiry Cycle with Feedback

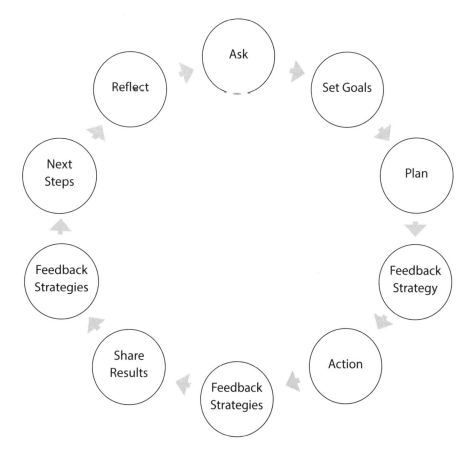

Feedback is a part of a larger framework that helps build and maintain classroom routines, promote vocabulary and accountable talk, and build acceptable guidelines surrounding positive communities of students who are able to learn to support each other's thinking and learning. Feedback is built and supported by our unique classroom communities and contexts for learning. As we move forward with the learning goals, we use feedback processes within the contexts of our classrooms.

Building Frameworks for Feedback

Frameworks for a successful feedback community are flexible and have the ability to evolve over time. They provide the boundaries that help organize the patterns of learning and communication within the classroom environment. They also set the stage for the evolution of effective feedback processes that will help drive the learning forward, not only from teacher to student but also from student to student and student to teacher.

Frameworks for feedback are not activities, although they are built through the collective strategies and activities you choose to implement in your classroom. They are the drivers of all of the aspects that go into the learning process.

The Feedback Frameworks Checklist on page 113 is a tool that you can use to keep track of what conventions you are implementing to create a feedback-friendly environment. It's a good starting point for your own organizational processes. It is meant as a checklist, but can be expanded to include anecdotal records. Having a separate sheet for each student may also be valuable.

Focus on Strengths

When facilitating a feedback-friendly classroom, it is important to focus on student strengths. It is essential to understand what you are looking for in terms of learning and make explicit what students should be looking for. We need to take the focus off the student and channel the focus onto the learning itself. When we make it specific, it also enables us to think forward to next steps for the students. In this sense, the feedback-friendly classroom can also be viewed as feed-forward–friendly.

Strategies that we can model for students when we are the ones passing feedback along must show students not merely what they have learned, but also that they did, in fact, learn! Make sure that students know when they did learn, even if they did not meet the success criteria or learning goals, yet.

Three Steps to Feedback: Student-to-Student

Provide guidelines for students to follow when they give feedback. The Three Steps to Feedback organizer on page 114 can be transferred to a chart paper, projected on the whiteboard via a document camera or mobile device, or printed out for students to practice on. When students are practicing, you can hand out an exemplar that you created, or an anonymous one from another year.

Students practice giving feedback in three steps:

1. Say something positive about the work.
2. Ask a question about the work.
3. Share a new idea you have learned based on the information in the work.

Conflicts and differences of opinions between teachers and students in terms of focus in the classroom can become pronounced when students are passive recipients of knowledge and feedback within the classroom. We can address conflicting ideas, goals, and opinions by moving students from being passive recipients of knowledge and feedback to co-creators of knowledge and feedback in the classroom.

Students should be familiar with class norms around feedback. See page 103.

Establish Group Norms

The co-creation of group norms with your class is essential for creating a feedback-friendly classroom. It is much more valuable for you to co-create them with your students than for me to provide you with what has worked for me.

Our schools and school boards have goals and objectives that we need to follow, in addition to the objectives that exist in our curriculum documents. To create a feedback-friendly classroom, you and your class need to agree on group norms that also fit in seamlessly with the other goals. They can change depending upon the goals that each school or classroom are hoping to accomplish. Here are examples of group norms established for a feedback-friendly classroom. Depending upon the age group, they can be modified for different levels of complexity and expression.

Academic Norms

- We will learn how to accept responsibility for our learning.
- We will work to identify things that are going well for other students, and focus on the tasks, not the person.
- We will seek information from other sources, including from our peers.

Socialization Norms

- We all need to work together and get along. We are interdependent in our learning.
- People create and establish communities to meet needs. A feedback-friendly community in our classroom will help us meet our learning needs.
- We appreciate the differences and similarities between ourselves and other learners.
- We will maintain attitudes about how we can help others.

Development Norms

- We will recognize when we are learning and that we are learning, even when we have not yet met the learning goal.
- We all have different backgrounds, cultures, and experiences. We might not be ready to learn the same way as someone else who has had more exposure to certain topics.

Set Goals

Goals not only set the standards that we want students to strive toward in the long term, they also define the processes we use to meet them. We need to base our feedback on the objectives and the processes as well.

What are your goals? Is it your goal for students to become independent thinkers? Is it your goal to improve literacy scores? What is the make-up of your class? Feedback ultimately depends on a host of variables that you will hone and harness to help reach your classroom goals.

The Goal-Setting: Class chart on page 115 helps show learning goals for your students and strategies to help achieve them. It could provide a way for you to see where you are going and what you will do to get there. This is flexible and can change, but it is useful to put a framework in place that will keep everyone on track together. This chart includes excellent questions that can start you on your journey to creating your feedback-friendly classroom.

It is important to identify your goals. They could include goals of the board, goals of the school, and learning goals for academics, socialization, and development. Ultimately, the needs and interests of the students inform the learning goals as well. Once you have your goals, think about the tasks that the students will be engaged in, whether summative or formative. Next, work backward from these tasks to determine the appropriate feedback strategies for your situation.

Goals are meaningless if they are meant only to gain compliance from the students. We need to help students set objectives based on goals and provide opportunities to interact with the objectives daily through feedback-friendly strategies. This gives students opportunities to measure continually and reflect upon their learning. Goals become more personalized and visible. See the Goal-Setting: Student template on page 115 for an organizational tool to fill out for each student.

The following are key characteristics that we need to keep in mind when setting learning goals for students and helping them to set new goals:

- Goals need to provide clarity and direction.
- Goals need to allow for skills and competencies to be demonstrated.
- Goals need to be interacted with, rehearsed, and visualized.
- Goals need to be the basis for key learning and feedback strategies.
- Goals need to guide feedback and assessment.
- Goals need to help teachers and students understand the difference between current learning behaviors and knowledge and what they need to do in the future.
- Goal planning will help students be successful.

Feedback and learning goals go hand in hand. Without goals, feedback is useless. Without feedback, the goals are also useless. For the feedback to be effective, it needs to be based in goals that closely meet the developmental levels of the learners. Once students have met their learning goals, they can go on to help give feedback to other students who need to meet the learning goals, or they can move on to other learning goals.

We need to guide our students in setting appropriate personal goals based on the broader learning goals in the classroom. Students play important roles in setting objectives because learning goals ultimately need to be valuable to the student. To this end, we allow for much leniency in feedback strategies that can be adapted to meet the overall goals in addition to our objectives. We also recognize that our students change from year to year, just as knowledge and society change. We need strategies to help students learn to evaluate continually their perspectives. The feedback for the objectives needs to be able to give information about how students are learning. This includes what they did well, what to improve, and what to do next.

We are always working together to set the curriculum goals. Feedback takes curriculum beyond the syllabus that teachers need to cover. It becomes about students setting and reaching goals together. Goal setting can be seen as the glue that links engagement and feedback together (Pollock, 2012).

Feedback-Friendly Language

Language, both written and oral, is the main vehicle that we use for giving, receiving, and seeking feedback. How students perceive feedback, and how teachers and students communicate feedback, will depend to a large extent on the accepted language and discourse of the classroom community. The feedback will be affected by different learner variables, including self-esteem, culture, and worldview.

We can build a language of the classroom that provides encouragement and motivation to our students about their learning. Because learning is inherently social, it will also be relational and emotional (Johnston); therefore, the language

It is helpful for students to see the objectives of their peers. This provides the social interactions by which students work together to reach objectives and goals, as it promotes conversation and appropriate peer feedback.

The language we use as teachers and the language we embed into the fabric of our classroom communities have a significant impact on student thinking. We must be careful with our wording to ensure that students are safe, able to take risks, and supported.

we use in feedback is essential to build strong learning communities within the classroom. The language that we teach in the classroom through vocabulary, accountable talk, etc., becomes woven into the culture of feedback that naturally occurs within the classroom.

Understanding language includes understanding how we use it, the prompts we use, our vocabulary, and how we can explicitly model and co-create the language with all learners. It may feel contrived at first—but it needs to become explicit and deliberate before it becomes automatic. Listening is an important first step toward being able to convey the language verbally. Also, linking words with pictures, hand gestures, and cues takes explicit practice through the strategies. The ultimate goal is to learn and use the language effectively for meaningful communication through the feedback process.

We can embed this language practice and usage into explicit strategies that students can use to seek, give, and receive feedback:

- Questions for clarification
- Paraphrasing
- Reflection on feedback
- Summarizing

Types of Language

We can use language to build growth mindsets, invite students to try to new things and try on new identities, make deeper connections, expand their imaginations, and reflect on their learning.

Language can be shared in templates, on anchor charts, or using Feedback Cards and Dice that you use as you progress through a particular unit of learning. They will change based on whether you are connecting them with academics, socialization, or development. If you are using them for academics, they will change based on whether you are using them for literacy, math processes, disciplinary thinking, or the scientific process; particularly the vocabulary will change. Therefore, these may be best filled in together as a class, either as a mind-mapping exercise or in talking circles. A new student from a different country may have a different question from a student who has lived in the community and gone to the school their whole career. Likewise a student from another family will have yet different questions. Culture, experiences, and prior knowledge all contribute to language shared in the learning environment.

Invitational Language

This is the language used to intentionally invite a student to learn. It includes listening and authenticity and also incorporates vocabulary and sentence starters. For instance, "let's" is a collaborative word that invites new and different perspectives. This simple word opens up possibilities about how else a problem could be solved.

Language for Responding

There are different types of strategies we can use and responses we can give. Brainstorming with students is effective because it also makes the language culturally responsive and collaborative. The curriculum documents unique to your province, state, or country should also be consulted for facilitating common language, but should not be the sole source for language used.

Feedback Cards are a strategy used to promote language development by socializing students' attention to patterns of language and thinking; see page 46 for more on Feedback Cards.

Language for Connections

Saying students' names helps anchor them as an important voice in the classroom.

This kind of language is at the heart of comprehension. It incorporates feedback-to-self, feedback-to-other, and feedback-to-world connections. We use this language to help students retrieve facts and concepts and apply them to new concepts. We also use this language to anchor students and keep them on track with the learning goals. Language for connections includes such phrases as "this reminds me of...," "this is just like...," and "this is different from..."

Language to Transfer Learning

Language to transfer learning encompasses the language students can use to help themselves and others transfer their learning to new situations and activities. It also includes the ability to synthesize differing opinions and ideas; it also helps students feel comfortable with struggles in their learning. With this language, students use vocabulary and words that promote reflection and metacognition. It also promotes the ability to make connections between different activities, problems, and learning. For example, asking fellow students about the different ways one activity is like the next is essential. Using "like" promotes comparisons, differences, similarities, contrasts. Questions like *What do I know about...?* and *What else is like this?* are used to transfer learning. Feedback Cards or Dice can help create the language for transferring learning.

Language to Expand Imagination

Imagination is expanded by questions like *How does _____ feel?* and discussions of how we feel and why.

This kind of language is important to help students think about new situations. They use it to ask questions and to wonder: *What would happen if...?* and *I wonder if...* Asking these questions of yourself or another student and carefully listening to the answer can help open up a dialogue that expands the imagination. It facilitates conversations that consider new situations and try on new ways of thinking. It allows students to create inquiries and informally converse about them with peers. This can help students to explore new solutions without having to suffer real consequences; i.e., getting a low grade, getting in trouble for a new behavior. Again, a trusting environment needs to be built so that students feel safe to take these kinds of risks of new thinking.

Language for Play

Vygotsky's learning theory states that social interaction and communities are central to students making meaning and learning. Using language for play helps the learning process, letting students try out language in different ways, experimenting to see its impact and usefulness in a social situation. Sometimes students will play with words that hurt someone else. In a feedback-friendly classroom, students can examine the effects of their words and consider effective strategies for meeting goals. Feedback Cards or Dice for socialization (see pages 82–83) or development (see page 92) can help cue these processes for students.

Language for Reflection

This is used as a way to validate one another's voices, to truly listen to one another; it also opens up new possibilities for taking learning in new directions.

Questioning Language

We have been conditioned in the traditional school system to believe that it is the teacher who asks the questions and has all the answers. However, if we transfer the authority for having the answers from the teacher to students, they can begin to take ownership for their questions. They can learn to ask other students, and other students will learn to listen to the patterns of questions and what kinds of counter-questions, ideas, answers, and other feedback can be shared as a response. Questions lead to discussion. Cooperative and student-centred learning includes project-based learning, makerspaces, content creation, and more. Therefore, strategies that ask better questions can help students focus on appropriate aspects of feedback. Our questions need not evoke emotion in our students. Further, our questions can be worded in ways that we do not have to make judgments about fellow students.

Nonverbal Language

We want to brainstorm with our students to create shared understandings in the classroom culture of what nonverbal language is. It incorporates the following questions:

- What does this look like?
- What does this sound like?
- What does this feel like?

These questions can be applied to academics, socialization, and development. In terms of development, these questions also connect very closely with self-regulation. Our youngest students are often less skilled in self-regulation than older students, but that is not always the case. All people develop at different times due to a host of reasons. Therefore, we will always need knowledgeable teachers to provide developmentally appropriate feedback to regulate the behaviors that lead to effective learning, growth, and development.

Nonverbal behavior is a big part of our everyday interactions and plays a role in relationship building. Body language and nonverbal communication have the ability to convey large amounts of information. We often use it to emphasize what we explicitly state verbally; however, what we do not say often gets neglected. In reality, verbal and nonverbal forms of communication are inseparable. They depend upon each other for meaning. Therefore, when we teach effective communication and feedback strategies, we also need to be mindful of the behaviors that accompany our words. Different cultures and families place greater emphasis on certain forms of feedback. For instance, pause times are valued in First Nations, Metis, and Inuit cultures, as they give space for deeper reflection and contemplation about learning and feedback.

As humans, we give nonverbal cues about how we feel. This is also true when we are giving or receiving feedback. It may be obvious to you as a teacher, but unknown to students about the feedback that they may be conveying with their nonverbal cues. Therefore, the use of strategies to bring awareness and attention to these forms of communication when giving and receiving feedback is important. Nonverbal cues can also be given as feedback for being open to receiving or giving feedback, starting or stopping a conversation. This includes those moments where we do not answer, or look at or turn away from another person. Positive nonverbal cues can include conserving our impulses, allowing for adequate pause times, offering respect, and meditating on new answers. It incorporates the times when we ask questions and then wait and listen. We are not using language because it is an appropriate time for our peers to think. This can also be used in one-on-one conferences when we ask students questions, in group work, or at any stage of the gradual release model; i.e., whole-class, shared, guided, and independent learning forums.

Assessment

Sometimes it can feel like the feedback-friendly classroom is pulling in the opposite direction from current assessment and reporting practices. Feedback-friendliness is a paradigm that does not fit with the assessment paradigms that have come to be associated with accountability. We cannot look at feedback simply as an either/or alternative to assessment. Instead, we can look at feedback as learning strategies and processes that enhance assessment.

Some of the different types of assessments that we have in our schools are categorized as

- assessment *for* learning
- assessment *of* learning
- assessment *as* learning

Assessment for, as, and of learning is still essential to student learning. It is still required for accountability to students and to all stakeholders to prove that learning is occurring.

The Observation Tool for Assessment on page 117 can be used for diagnostic and formative assessment. It can be used to organize your observations of learning as it pertains to diagnostic and formative assessment. A place to write the date, subject, and student and teacher information can be valuable in that it makes the record specific.

Triangulation of Assessment Data

We should never look only at the final products when making assessment decisions. Remember that we are using feedback as a learning strategy, not just as a tool that accompanies assessment. Moreover, as teachers we do not want to be the sole people in control of the feedback that gets shared. We want to acknowledge everyone's role and responsibility in working toward the learning goals. We want to promote conversations and help students to engage in observation strategies that promote learning.

The Assessment Triangle

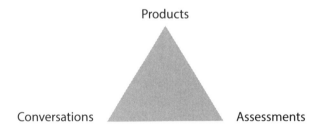

We want to facilitate the kinds of conversations that students need to become deeper thinkers, to take other points of view into consideration, and to share what they already know. There is great information to be harnessed about our teaching and instructional practices from the conversations and relationships in the classroom. Triangulation of assessment is a tool that can integrate assessment paradigms with feedback-friendly processes within the classroom toward new ways of thinking, organizing, and behaving with learning strategies.

Feedback Triangulation Template for Students and Teachers

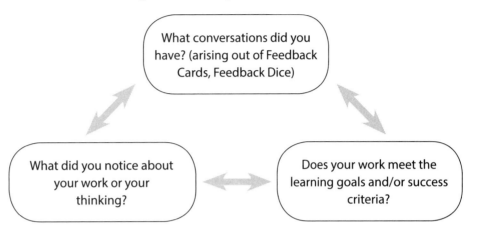

Assessing Conversations and Observations

A spreadsheet can be used to tabulate conversations, observations, and products. Then responses can be coded, patterns can be identified, and pedagogy can be appropriately adapted to meet the needs of the learners.

Observation Activity: The Observed and the Observer

In this activity, the observer is closely monitoring the conversation or activity/ strategy, e.g., Think–Pair–Feedback.

A few questions to keep in mind before you begin:

- Have you effectively introduced your activity/strategy to the class to discuss what they are working on and observing?
- Have you defined the focus of the observations?
- Have you discussed the learning goals they are connecting to?

Checklist for Observed Student(s)

☐ Students have been able to share their observations first.
☐ Students have had time to reflect and communicate information and ideas.

What did you hear about the observations?	
Did you have time to reflect on this information?	
Is there anything you are still confused about?	
What are your next steps?	

Student conversations can be recorded and listened to again later. Students and teachers can also listen together as a great way to strengthen the reliability of the feedback and learning taking place.

Checklist for Student Observer
☐ I saw my classmate doing the activity.
☐ I heard my classmate doing the activity.

What did you see?	
What did you hear?	
What do you still wonder?	

Assessing Products

How can we assess products of learning in feedback-friendly ways? This part of the triangulation of data is evaluative and, therefore, should be conducted by the teacher. In a feedback-friendly classroom, students should not be required to evaluate each other, but they can be positive and purposeful with Feedback Cards and Feedback Dice (see pages 46 and 49). As educators, we are the ones ultimately accountable for increasing student achievement; however, when students have the option to always improve, and when peers are given cues and strategies to use positively, the whole classroom can play a role in increasing student achievement.

As we empower students to be a part of the process, we are teaching them to think and act and speak in ways that provide consistent quality feedback for every class, every student, and every day. Students love to be recognized for what they know. If we harness the power of our peers and other audiences effectively, then we are helping students to look toward other strengths. A culture of feedback is maintained by a classroom of experts with the goal of helping students to become better thinkers. This cannot be done by assessing products alone.

Portfolios are collections of student work. I like to use portfolios in addition to journal writing as a metacognitive task for students to engage in self-reflection and give themselves valuable feedback for learning. For example, portfolios are an excellent way to help students address the incremental beliefs we have about intelligence, and demonstrate cognitive, emotional and behavioral improvements. E-portfolios can be organized into sections to demonstrate how far we have progressed in terms of socialization, academics, and development. This promotes a growth mindset because the emphasis is not on the grades or on learning as an end in and of itself. It is instead a way to demonstrate and make visible just how far a student has come during the year.

Self- and Peer-Assessment

Self-assessment is an important component part of the feedback process. Students need to understand how to accurately self-assess. This is very difficult, especially if the criteria are not made explicit, modelled, and regularly practiced within the classroom. Criteria are crucial to help anchor students who are giving, receiving, and seeking accurate feedback from the social environment and interchanges within the classroom. It is recommended that we allow students to self-assess only the process, and not the final result. For instance, within this process of helping students self-assess, student learning is facilitated by following simple procedures and tasks:

It is important that students understand that any product can be improved, and they are allowed to improve it if they would like.

Because students need to interact with their notes in order to be truly reflective (Pollock, 2012), portfolios and journals are excellent strategies to help students engage in self-feedback.

1. Provide exemplars: in the form of role plays, written work, videos, demonstrations, projects, etc. Exemplars also help model to your students what feedback interactions look like within the classroom. Some of the criteria we can explicitly draw attention to are what the interactions look like, feel like; if they are flexible, goal-oriented, consistent, focused, and positive (Marchand, 2014).

2. Have students generate a list of success criteria: things they think are necessary for assessing the task at hand. The list can be translated into a rubric for students to use as they are working on their task. Success criteria can be used formatively to help students develop the skills for doing their work, and also help clarify the standards for giving, receiving, and seeking quality feedback about the learning processes as students move toward them.

3. Have students practice with the assessment rubric. There is a difference between students recognizing criteria of a feedback-friendly classroom and actually putting it to practice. On a daily basis, depending on the task, students can engage in feedback strategies (see Chapters 4 through 7), interacting with the rubric:

- They can underline with colored pencils the key elements in the rubric they believe they demonstrated.
- Next, they can demonstrate evidence of meeting that criteria.
- If students are unable to demonstrate certain criteria, or elements of criteria, they need to reflect, record, and share how they could.

Perceived and real support from peers also has an impact on school engagement and achievement (Furrer, 2003). A child's sense of relatedness, or feeling of connectedness, plays a very important role in academic motivation and performance. Research suggests that it be a school priority to build the quality of student relationships (Furrer, 2003), so quality peer assessment practices are beneficial for building feedback-friendly classrooms.

Tracking Templates

Tracking templates are valuable for teachers and students to keep track of feedback and learning. It is an organizational strategy. All feedback does not have to be recorded, but sometimes it is very valuable to have a record. At report card time, it is always important to have your findings at the ready. The templates on pages 36–39 can be beneficial to track the learning.

One-Point/Three-Column Rubric

Assess students informally with a checklist or an online form while they are engaged in discussion in a Think–Pair–Feedback activity.

In a one-column rubric, there is space for students to input the criteria the class decides upon. Or you can enter the criteria and print off a copy for each student. At any point in the learning process, you can have students interact with the feedback using one of the feedback strategies and have students self-assess according to a rubric like this. See page 118 for a template for a One-Point Rubric.

Checklist

Number the success criteria determined together as a class, then use a quick checklist to check off if they were met or not; see Success Criteria Checklist template on page 119. Use the notes section to discuss criteria that were not met and how they would be addressed differently in the future.

Sending Feedback Home

As educators, we need to model what feedback looks like for our students, staff, parents, and community. We give feedback in writing, orally, or through the process of modelling to show students what it looks like, sounds like, and feels like; we model how to effectively share ideas while still honoring the ideas of our peers; we honor choice and the use of students' ideas to drive learning, while determining how much choice students can actually handle. Just as we begin by modelling feedback to our learners, so must we consider how we will model the feedback to parents, families, and communities.

Feedback Information Night

We often offer information nights to parents: literacy events, tech events, back-to-school events, and many more. Consider holding a Feedback Information night to make parents aware of the importance of feedback and how you will be implementing it within your classroom. This can go a long way toward setting the stage for a successful school year and eliciting parent support for strategies they might not be aware of. See page 120 for an invitation to send home with your students.

Start by creating a summary sheet that explains the importance of feedback and some of the different strategies that students will engage in. See the Feedback Summary on page 121 for a reproducible copy of an information sheet.

Sending Feedback Cards Home

Feedback Cards (see page 46) can be sent home as a valuable homework alternative. Families can help students work to reflect and obtain feedback and give appropriate feedback to learners. This process can elicit information about how parents and students understand the material. There are worksheets and templates that students can fill out, or they could take a picture and upload to an e-portfolio to share in class. The cards can provide systematic ways of looking at homework and communicating about learning during the school day. Feedback Cards to be shared at home could outline various strategies that focus on what students learned at school:

Learning Goal	Question I had	Question I still have
Question from Home	Picture of Learning	What I still need from my teacher

Feedback Frameworks Checklist

	Feedback for Socialization	Feedback for Academics	Feedback for Development
Language			
Routines			
Learning Goals			
Observation			
Questioning			
Routines			
Objects for Learning			
Comprehension Strategies			
Learning Strategies			
Sharing			

Pembroke Publishers © 2015 *The Feedback-Friendly Classroom* by Deborah McCallum ISBN 978-1-55138-304-0

Three Steps to Feedback

3 Steps	Feedback
1. Say something positive	
2. Ask a question	
3. Share a new idea (*If…, then…; Have you thought of this?; This is something I have learned!*)	

Pembroke Publishers © 2015 *The Feedback-Friendly Classroom* by Deborah McCallum ISBN 978-1-55138-304-0

Goal-Setting: Class

	What am I going to learn?	What do I already know?	How will I get there?	What do I do next?
Classroom Learning	Review learning goals, success criteria, exemplars, the feedback process	Use diagnostic assessments, reflections; Have students make connections, use strategies to interact with the learning goals, success criteria, exemplars, language	Strategies Language	Interacting with the feedback to make new decisions, plans; use feedback to create a dialogue
Strategies	See Strategies Chapters	See Strategies Chapters	See Strategies Chapters	See Strategies Chapters
Next Steps	Next learning goal, success criteria	Assessment, reflection on feedback	Set new goals	Plan for moving forward

Pembroke Publishers © 2015 *The Feedback-Friendly Classroom* by Deborah McCallum ISBN 978-1-55138-304-0

Goal-Setting: Student

Name	Goals	Learning Needs	Interests	Tasks	Feedback Strategy

Pembroke Publishers © 2015 *The Feedback-Friendly Classroom* by Deborah McCallum ISBN 978-1-55138-304-0

Observation Tool for Assessment

Date	Assessment of	Subject	Student	Teacher
	Knowledge			
	Understanding			
	Communication			
	Application			

Pembroke Publishers © 2015 *The Feedback-Friendly Classroom* by Deborah McCallum ISBN 978-1-55138-304-0

One-Point Rubric

Explicit Evidence: How I met the criteria	Criteria	Reflection: How I would meet the criteria next time

Pembroke Publishers © 2015 *The Feedback-Friendly Classroom* by Deborah McCallum ISBN 978-1-55138-304-0

Success Criteria Checklist

Success Criteria	Met	Not Met
1		
2		
3		
4		
5		
6		
7		

For the numbered criteria that you did not meet, please explain why, and what you will do next time to improve.

Criterion # ____. Notes: _____

Criterion # ____. Notes: _____

Criterion # ____. Notes: _____

Criterion # ____. Notes: _____

Pembroke Publishers © 2015 *The Feedback-Friendly Classroom* by Deborah McCallum ISBN 978-1-55138-304-0

Invitation

Welcome to our Feedback Information Night!

Come and learn how we will be using feedback this year to support learning in the 21st Century! Our goal is to create a Feedback-Friendly Classroom where quality feedback is built into the culture of our classroom. Learn how you can support your children at home too!

Date: _____

Time: _____

Location: _____

Pembroke Publishers © 2015 *The Feedback-Friendly Classroom* by Deborah McCallum ISBN 978-1-55138-304-0

Feedback Summary

What is a Feedback-Friendly Classroom?

This year, our goal is to create a Feedback-Friendly classroom. Did you know that an estimated 80% of the feedback that students receive in the classroom comes from their peers, and most of that feedback is either not helpful or incorrect? This year, we will be using high-quality, research-proven strategies to help students integrate meaningful feedback into our everyday classroom interactions to promote learning.

Feedback Basics

- Feedback is an important part of assessment.
- Feedback is a process that goes beyond assessment.
- Quality feedback can increase learning and growth mindsets.
- Feedback is not graded on an assessment.
- Feedback incorporates key skills that students need moving forward in the 21st century.

You can support your child by

- Using feedback-friendly language.
- Looking beyond the grade.
- Promoting growth mindsets.

We can support you by

- Providing Feedback Cards for home and explaining how to use them.
- Making feedback visible.
- Maintaining communication.

Pembroke Publishers © 2015 *The Feedback-Friendly Classroom* by Deborah McCallum ISBN 978-1-55138-304-0

References

Ahwee, E.A. (2004) "The Hidden and Null Curriculums: An experiment in collective educational biography" *Educational Studies (American Educational Studies Association), 35*(1), 25–43.

Anastasyia, L., & Smith, J. K. (2009) "Effects of Differential Feedback on Students' Examination Performance" *Journal of Experimental Psychology, 15*(4), 319–333.

Andrade, H. D. (2008) "Putting Rubrics to the Test: The effect of a model, criteria generation, and rubric-referenced self-assessment on Elementary school students' writing" *Education Measurement: Issues and Practice*, 3–13.

Beck, C. D. (2015) *Easy and Effective Professional Development: The Power of Peer Observation to Improve Teaching*. New York, NY: Routledge.

Black, Paul, & Dylan, Wiliam. "Inside the Black Box: Raising standards through classroom assessment" *Phi Delta Kappan* 80.2 (1998): 139–48.

Bronwen, C., Moreland, J., & Otrel-Cass, K. (2013) *Expanding Notions of Assessment for Learning: Inside science and technology primary classrooms*. Rotterdam, NL: SensePublishers.

Brookhart, S. (2011) "Tailoring Feedback" *The Education Digest*, 33–36.

Dweck, C. (2006) *Mindset: The New Psychology of Success*. New York, NY: Ballantine Books.

Furrer, C. & Skinner, E. (2003) "Sense of Relatedness as a Factor in Children's Academic Engagement and Performance" *Journal of Educational Psychology, 95*(1), 148–162.

Gersten, R., Baker, S., & Edwards, L. (2001) "Teaching Expressive Writing to Students with Learning Disabilities: A Meta-Analysis" *The Elementary School Journal, 101*(3), 251–266.

Hattie, J. (2009) *Visible Learning: A synthesis of over 800 Meta-Analyses relating to achievement*. New York, NY: Routledge.

Hattie, J. (2012) *Visible Learning for Teachers: Maximizing impact on learning*. New York, NY: Routledge.

Hayes, D. (2008) "Centres and Perspectives: Soliciting Learner Feedback in Japan" *Innovation in Language Learning and Teaching, 2*(2), 152–173.

Hughes, J. Z. (2006) "Peer Assessments of Normative and Individual Teacher–Student Support Predict Social Acceptance and Engagement Among Low-achieving Children" *Journal of School Psychology, 43*, 447–463.

Johnston, P. (2004) *Choice Words*. Portland, ME: Stenhouse Publishers.

Marchand, G., & Furrer, C. (2014) "Formative, Informative, and Summative Assessment: The relationship among curriculum-based measurement of reading, classroom engagement, and reading performance" *Psychology in the Schools, 51*(7), 659–676.

Martin, A. (2015) "Growth Approaches to Academic Development: Research into academic trajectories and growth assessment, goals, and mindsets" *British Journal of Educational Psychology, 85*(2), 133-137.

Masters, G. N. (2014) "Towards a Growth Mindset in Assessment" *Practically Primary, 19*(2). Retrieved from http://go.galegroup.com.myaccess.library.utoronto.ca/ps/i.do?id=GALE%7CA379640511&v=2.1&u=utoronto_main&it=r&p=AONE&sw=w&asid=658279d9e85853da5d39410ca7f0be5a

Nilson, L. (2003) "Improving Student Peer Feedback" *College Teaching, 51*(1).

Nuthall, G. (2007) *The Hidden Lives of Learners*. Wellington, NZ: New Zealand Council for Educational Research.

Ornstein, A. C. (2013) *Curriculum: Foundations, principles, and issues, 6th Edition*. New York, NY: Pearson.

Pollock, J.E. (2012) *Feedback: The hinge that joins teaching & learning*. Thousand Oaks, CA: Sage Publications.

Regan, K. M. (2013) "Cultivating Self-Regulation for Students With Mild Disabilities: What's up?" *Intervention in School and Clinic 4, 49*(3), 164–173.

Rotman School of Management. (n.d.). *Integrative Thinking Explained*. Retrieved from https://www.rotman.utoronto.ca/FacultyAndResearch/ResearchCentres/DesautelsCentre/Integrative%20Thinking/New%20to%20Integrative%20Thinking.aspx

Ryan, R., & Deci, E. (2000) "Intrinsic and Extrinsic Motivations: Classic definitions and new directions" *Contemporary Educational Psychology, 25*(1), 54–67.

Shanker, S. (2013). *Calm, Alert, and Learning: Classroom strategies for self-regulation*. Don Mills, ON: Pearson.

Smith, M. H. (2009) "Orchestrating Discussions" *Mathematics Teaching in Middle School*.

Sutton, R., Hornsey, M., & Douglas, K. (2011) *Feedback: The communication of praise, criticism, and advice*. Retrieved from Visible Learning Plus: http://visiblelearningplus.com/sites/default/files/Feedback%20article.pdf

The Quality Assurance Agency for Higher Education (2009) *Enhancing Practice*. Retrieved from Quality Enhancement Themes: Transforming assessment and feedback: http://www.enhancementthemes.ac.uk/docs/publications/transforming-assessment-and-feedback.pdf?sfvrsn=12

van den Bergh, L. R. (2013) "Feedback During Active Learning: Elementary school teachers' beliefs and perceived problems" *Educational Studies, 39*(4), 428–430.

Zimmerman, B. (2002) "Becoming a Self-regulated Learner: An overview" *Theory into Practice, 41*, 64–72.

Index